Study Guide

to accompany

Jones • Wood • Borstelmann • May • Ruiz

CREATED EQUAL

A History of the United States

Volume One

Third Edition

William Pelz

Elgin Community College

PEARSON

Longman

New York Boston San Francisco
London Toronto Sydney Tokyo Singapore Madrid
Mexico City Munich Paris Cape Town Hong Kong Montreal

Study Guide to accompany Jones/Wood/Borstelmann/May/Ruiz, *Created Equal: A History of the United States, Volume One, Third Edition*

Copyright ©2009 Pearson Education, Inc.

ISBN: 0-205-61844-8

ISBN-13: 978-0-205-61844-6

1 2 3 4 5 6 7 8 9 10–OPM–11 10 09 08

CONTENTS

Chapter 1
First Founders

Learning Objectives:

After reading Chapter 1, you should be able to:

1. Discuss the origins of the first peoples to live in America.
2. Detail the story of the Kennewick Man and explain the most recent evidence as to the origins of the first inhabitants of America.
3. Understand how human groups adapted to changes in the climate.
4. Detail the Mesoamerican Empires that existed from A.D. 300 to 900.
5. Analyze why the great urban centers of Peru and Mesoamerica had no northern counterparts.
6. Explain the significance of the Cahokia and Moundville.
7. Discuss early European travel to the Western Hemisphere.
8. Understand the reasons behind the beginnings of globalization.
9. Analyze the reasons for the mistakes that led Columbus to mistake America for Asia.
10. Comprehend the importance of the Spanish devastation of the Indies.
11. Understand how the Spanish conquest of the Aztecs was achieved.
12. Discuss the various European expeditions that came to America in the sixteenth century.
13. Analyze how the Protestant Reformation affected America.
14. Discuss the reasons for increased English attention to America.

Time Line

14,000 years ago
Early Paleo-Indians in Florida and Pennsylvania regions and in Chile

13,900 to 12,900 year ago
Clovis hunters spread across North America

10,000 to 3,000 years ago
Archaic Indians flourish in diverse settings

300 A.D.
Rise of Mayan Culture

800 A.D.
Moche Empire collapsed

1000 A.D.
Vikings reached North American coast

1492
Columbus reached Hispaniola

1497
John Cabot reached Newfoundland

1522
Cortes conquered the Aztec Empire

1533
Francisco Pizarro conquered Incas in Peru

1534
Jacques Cartier reached the Gulf of the St. Lawrence

1537
Hernando de Soto granted right to conquer Florida by Spanish crown

1590
Roanoke colony site found deserted

I. Ancient America

A. The Question of Origins

The ancestors of Indian societies have lived in America for at least 14,000 years. Although scientific research increasingly documents the general story of human origins and migration, nothing can diminish the powerful creation stories passed down from ancestors. These serve an important cultural purpose. Modern humans developed in Africa, but 50,000 to 70,000 years ago, they began to migrate. Bands of northern hunters migrated east across Siberia in search of game. Arriving at the Bering land bridge, then exposed because of Arctic ice caps, some hunters made the trip from Asia to America. As the climate warmed, the land bridge was flooded while passages to the south opened up. Scholars suspect that the newcomers followed game southward, reaching the tip of South America in a few thousand years.

Some scientists have found evidence that some peoples may have traveled from Asia to America by sea. While it is unclear whether humans took to boats before as well as after arriving, the DNA evidence shows that the first population of America came primarily from Asia. Recent discoveries suggest the presence of predecessors to Clovis people. Small groups may have used simple boats more than 14,000 years ago on a route along the coast of the North Pacific rim and traveled down the coastline to ultimately reach South America.

B. The Archaic World

Some 10,000 years ago, the Paleo-Indian eras gave way to the different Archaic era as climate changes and more than 100 of America's largest species disappeared. Human groups had to adapt to new conditions. Although genetically similar, far-flung bands of Archaic Indians developed diverse cultures in reaction to very different environments. A few early languages branched into numerous language families, and similar cultural variations emerged in everything from lifestyle to spiritual beliefs.

All of this difference was a reflection of local conditions. Some developed into elaborate social arrangements while others were experiments that were later modified or discarded. Priests often appeared near the top of a developing class hierarchy that was unknown in hunting and gathering societies. Slavery was also beginning to become a fact of life.

C. The Rise of Maize Agriculture

The various Archaic American groups had one important thing in common: their lack of domesticated animals. They did have dogs and, in the Andes, llamas, but there remained no other large mammal that could give humans milk, meat, hides, or hauling power. With regard to the domestication of plants, Americans had more options. Unlike wheat in Eurasia which offered a high yield from the start, American crops like maize took thousands of years to develop into a productive food source. Across parts of South America, people learned to cultivate root crops such as potatoes. Also, in Mesoamerica inhabitants began to cultivate squash, beans, and maize (corn). These foods are an effective complement to one another in terms of diet.

About 3,000 years ago, the Olmecs emerged as the first of several powerful Mesoamerican cultures. They developed a complex calendar, revered the jaguar, and built large mounds and pyramids. They traded widely with people across Mesoamerica and passed on their cultural traits, as shown by the possibility that they influenced the Poverty Point culture of the lower Mississippi River.

II. A Thousand Years of Change: A.D. 500 to 1500

A. Valleys of the Sun: The Mesoamerican Empires

The Mayans controlled an area half the size of Texas in what is today southern Mexico, Guatemala, Honduras, and El Salvador between A.D. 300 and 900. Getting their elaborate calendar from the Olmecs as well as other cultural traits, the Mayans also built huge stone temples and conducted ritual blood sacrifices to their gods. The Mayans declined mysteriously as did the Moches in Peru and were replaced by the people of Teotihuacan, who in turn were replaced by the Toltecs and then the Aztecs.

The Aztecs migrated to the valley of Mexico in the twelfth century. Although they were at first looked down on as uncultured, the Aztecs rose quickly to power because of skillful alliances and military might. They founded their capital of Tenochtitlan on a swampy island in Lake Texococ, and by the 1400s, the Aztecs had transformed their city into an imposing urban center. The Aztecs were molded by hardship, pessimism, and violence, seeing themselves as living in a final human era destined to end in cataclysm. Launching fierce wars against their neighbors, the Aztecs demanded tribute and took prisoners who they then sacrificed at pyramid temples to please their gods. This harsh treatment of conquered peoples left the Aztecs vulnerable to external attack.

B. The Anasazi: Chaco Canyon and Mesa Verde

Although there are no counterparts to the great urban centers of Peru and Mesoamerica farther north, three clearly different cultures were well-established in the American Southwest by A.D. 500. The Mogollons lived in sunken pit houses in what is now eastern Arizona and southern New Mexico. Their neighbors to the west, the Hohokams, constructed extensive canal and floodgate systems to irrigate their fields. To the north, where Utah and Colorado now meet Arizona and New Mexico, lived the Anasazi, or "ancient ones," and violence and warfare played an important part in their life. In the end, however, environmental changes exerted the greatest force as a drought gripped the Colorado Plateau for half a century after 1130.

C. The Mississippians: Cahokia and Moundville

The Hopewell people had prospered in the Mississippi Valley for the first 500 years A.D. Their trading laid the groundwork for later, larger mound-building societies, known as the Mississippian cultures. Living in southern Ohio and western Illinois, the Hopewell established a network of trade that covered much of North America. Spreading after A.D. 500, a more elaborate and widespread culture flourished for six centuries after A.D. 900. Maize went from a marginal crop to a central staple, and by 1300, maize and bean agriculture reached all the way to the Iroquois people around Lake Ontario. As food supplies expanded, Indian peoples began to settle in these fertile areas, and developed patterns of bureaucracy and hierarchy. With increased productivity, commercial and religious elites gained greater control over farmers.

Mississippian mound-building cultures were diverse and widespread. Although much is still not known about them, the largest complex developed at Cahokia in the floodplain below where the Illinois and Missouri rivers flow into the Mississippi. Cahokia rose quickly around A.D. 1050, as small villages were reorganized into a strong regional chiefdom. The centralized elite controlled food, labor, trade, and religion, as well as life and death, as shown by the evidence of human sacrifice. Cahokia declined and other regional chiefdoms arose along other rivers. The most important appears to be Moundville in west-central Alabama, which remained powerful until around 1400. For a thousand years, societies had risen by linking agriculture and trade only to decline and fall upon reaching environmental limits. A river drying up could help destroy an entire way of life.

III. Linking the Continents

A. Oceanic Travel: The Norse and the Chinese

Around A.D. 1000, Scandinavian Vikings explored and then settled a region near the Gulf of St. Lawrence that they called Vinland. A tiny colony of 160 Vikings lived and grazed livestock in Vinland for several years until driven out by native peoples. For centuries, the Norse contact was known only from oral tradition, but recent research has discovered evidence of a Viking settlement in northern Newfoundland. In fact, these settlements were little known by native

Americans and had little impact on their societies. The Viking settlements in Greenland lasted much longer, possibly for three centuries, until climate change, soil erosion, and a slump in trade in Europe caused by the plague finally ended the last settlements by 1450.

Europeans were vaguely aware of the existence of the Chinese Empire, particularly after Marco Polo recounted his visit there in the 1270s in his *Travels*. Polo told of many wondrous things, such as spices that could preserve meat and rocks that burned like wood (coal). When Islamic power cut off the Silk Road, the Europeans looked for other ways to reach this far-off land.

It was China that first mastered ocean sailing, not Europe. In 1281, Kublai Khan sailed 4,500 ships in an attempt to invade Japan, only to have the invasion wrecked by a huge typhoon. Chinese overseas expansion reached its height in the early fifteenth century, as the brilliant Admiral Zheng He led seven large fleets to the Indian Ocean and as far as the East African coast. Then China turned from overseas trade and grew socially inward, with officials even destroying the log books of earlier voyages. Instead of China shaping oceanic trade and the fate of North America, it fell to the small country of Portugal to emerge as the leader in maritime exploration in the fifteen century.

B. Portugal and the Beginnings of Globalization

Portugal sat at the crossroads of the Mediterranean trade and the coastal traffic of northern Europe. With the failure of the crusades to defeat Islam, Christian traders dreamed of reaching China by sailing around Africa. Even if this was not possible, it was thought that exploration south of the Sahara Desert could discover the extent of Islamic influence and might open up new trade or produce converts to Christianity. For these efforts to succeed, there was a need for determined leadership, which was provided by Prince Henry (1394-1460), later known as Henry the Navigator. Henry's ships pushed along the African coast, reaching as far south as Sierra Leone in his lifetime. One major result of this push was the discovery of three island groups— Canaries, Madeiras, and Azores—off the Northwest coast of Africa, which sparked an overseas colonization process. In addition, by the 1440s, Portuguese mariners were seizing Western African coastal residents and importing them to Europe as slaves.

C. Looking for the Indies: da Gama and Columbus

Portuguese exploration was rewarded in 1487 when Bartolomeu Dias rounded the southernmost part of Africa, proving that it was possible to sail to India from Lisbon. A decade later, Vasco da Gama successfully sailed to India and returned with a ship loaded with pepper and cinnamon. There was now a southeastern sea route to Asia.

Portugal's rival Spain gambled on finding a profitable westward route to the Indies. In 1492, as they were expelling Moslems and Jews from their kingdom, King Ferdinand and Queen Isabella sponsored a voyage by Christopher Columbus. With 90 men and three small ships, Columbus sailed west and finally found what he thought was an island only ten days from the mainland of China. In fact, this island was part of the Bahamas and the island he thought was Japan was actually Cuba. Columbus's mistake flowed from his belief that the world was 25 percent smaller than it actually is, a belief that contradicted both ancient estimates and most contemporary theories.

D. In the Wake of Columbus: Competition and Exchange

After Columbus's return, the Pope issued a decree dividing the world between Spain and Portugal; the former was given the right to search for a western route to Asia while the latter could have a monopoly in developing the path around southern Africa. Brazil happened to be within the area granted to Portugal so it quickly claimed this territory but otherwise left further Atlantic exploration to others.

Both Spain and England acted quickly, with Columbus returning to Hispaniola with 1,200 men aboard 17 ships. The English king, Henry VII, licensed John Cabot, an Italian navigator, to search for a northern passage to China. Cabot reached Newfoundland thinking he had reached Asia but died on a return voyage and Henry VII lacked the resources to follow up this first English-sponsored attempt. After thousands of years of separation, the world was becoming linked. The Europeans brought seeds, diseases, insects, and birds, plants, and animals. They sent back corn, potatoes, pumpkins, chili peppers, tobacco, cacao, pineapples, sunflowers, turkeys, and maybe syphilis. The world would never be the same.

IV. Spain Enters the Americas

A. The Devastation of the Indies

Spanish conquest of the West Indies brought ecological and human disaster. The newcomers killed and enslaved native peoples while Spanish livestock trampled or devoured native gardens. European diseases were the worst imports and ravaged native peoples. The result was that 19 out of 20 native people died within a generation. This near-extinction led devout Catholics to protest the loss of potential converts, and Dominican friars who reached Cuba in 1510 denounced Spanish brutality as sinful. In addition, the loss of population led the Spanish to import slaves from Africa to replace the dead native workers, while the decimation of the islands pushed the Spanish to intensify their search for new conquests.

B. The Spanish Conquest of the Aztec

Realizing that the Gulf of Mexico provided no passage to Asia, the Spanish sent Ferdinand Magellan to sail around South America. Although his crew nearly starved crossing the Pacific, and Magellan and a number of his men were killed by natives in the Philippines, one of his ships made it back to Spain, becoming the first vessel to circumnavigate the globe.

In 1519, Hernan Cortes, a Spanish *conquistador,* or soldier, reached the edge of what he realized was a mighty empire. The Aztec emperor Moctezuma reacted to news of the strangers with uncertainty, since ominous signs indicated this event might be the return of a god. The emperor sent gifts of precious objects and gold to Cortes, which only revealed to the Spanish forces the wealth of the Aztecs.

Although Cortes had fewer than 600 men, they had guns and horses, which were unknown to the Aztecs. In addition, their ruthless style of warfare, in which the Spanish killed as many of their enemies as possible, shocked the Aztecs, who had also sought to take captives. The Aztec practice of human sacrifice enraged the Spaniards, and the Indian peoples oppressed by the empire became willing allies of the newcomers. While the Aztec leadership proved weak, Cortes was decisive. Still, had it not been for the smallpox epidemic that arrived with the Europeans, the task of conquering the Aztecs would have been more daunting. Cortes renamed the Aztec capital Mexico City and claimed the entire region as New Spain.

C. Magellan and Cortez Prompt New Searches

The fall of the Aztecs led the Spanish to hope for further riches in the Americas, while the length of Magellan's voyage encouraged the search for a shorter route to Asia. Spanish raiders under Francisco Pizarro attacked the Inca Empire in Peru and, assisted again by smallpox, sacked the capital for its gold. Various other expeditions were launched to find either new routes to Asia or American gold to plunder. Neither Cortes nor Balboa found a water passage near the equator that directly linked the Atlantic and Pacific Oceans.

D. Three New Views of North America

Although they were competitors, the enterprises of Jacques Cartier, Hernando de Soto and Francisco Vasquez de Coronado made the ten years after 1534 the most important decade in early European exploration of North America. The French, under Jacques Cartier, arrived at the Gulf of St. Lawrence and bartered for furs with the natives. Returning the following year, Cartier ventured into Canada. Although he failed to find the valuable minerals he sought, Cartier was the first of the French expeditions that challenged Spain's exclusive claim to North America.

In 1537, the Spanish Crown granted Hernando de Soto the right to conquer Florida. For the next four years, de Soto pillaged Indian villages in search of gold before dying of a fever after reaching beyond the Mississippi River. His demoralized followers escaped downstream to the Gulf of Mexico. Greater than the direct destruction wrought by de Soto was the horror of the epidemic sicknesses he left in his wake.

At the same time, in the Southwest, Francisco Vasquez de Coronado set out from northwestern Mexico in search of fabulous wealth. He found the pueblos of the Zunis but no significant wealth. The Spanish troops imposed a huge burden on the Pueblo Indians by demanding food and burning down any village that resisted. In a plan to rid themselves of these oppressors, the Indians told the Spanish of a far-off land of countless treasures. They recruited a Plains Indian and had him lead the Spanish out into the Great Plains. When Coronado realized that the legendary city of wealth was a small Kansas Indian village, he had the guide killed and returned to New Spain.

V. The Protestant Reformation Plays Out in America

A. Reformation and Counter-Reformation in Europe

Following Martin Luther's demands for religious reforms, the years of the sixteenth century saw Europe split into Catholic and Protestant camps. The Protestant Reformation coincided with the desire of European monarchs to distance their power from the authority of the Pope. Now religious hostilities would spill over into the Americas.

B. Competing Powers Lay Claim to Florida

Jealous of the dazzling wealth Spain expropriated from the New World, France sent raiders to capture Spanish ships returning from Mexico. French Protestants, or Huguenots, led the way in efforts to colonize Brazil and Florida. The Portuguese uprooted the French in Brazil while Spain ousted the Huguenots from Florida. Although the French were defeated, English adventurers began challenging Spanish domination in the Caribbean and along the southeast coast of North America.

C. The Background of English Expansion

After 1550, Henry VIII of England used the wealth he had seized from the Catholic Church to add 85 ships to the Royal Navy. The merchant fleet expanded at the same time as did the English population. When Europe's woolen textile market collapsed in 1551, merchants looked for new forms of foreign commerce. They need new markets for their goods. Expanding in all directions, England established contact with Russia but failed to find a northeast route to China. The English also challenged the Portuguese monopoly of the African trade and began to engage in the slave trade. While Spain was at first successful in driving Sir Francis Drake out of Mexican waters, the English captain continued to attack Spanish shipping and helped defeat King Philip's Spanish Armada in 1588.

Anti-Catholic propagandists made Drake a national English hero and emphasized the brutality of the Spanish against the Indians, although the English were little better. When Sir Humphrey Gilbert died while attempting to establish a colony in Newfoundland, his half-brother, Sir Walter Raleigh, obtained the right to establish an English colony in North America.

D. Lost Colony: The Roanoke Experience

Raleigh's three attempts to establish a colony failed quickly. In 1587, John White led a third English expedition to North America and set up at Roanoke Island. When White returned after three years from England, where he had gone for supplies, he found the settlement deserted, with nothing but the word *Croatoan* carved on a post. The fate of the colony has never been determined.

Identification

Explain the significance of each of the following:

1. Atlatl:

2. Incas:

3. Mississippians:

4. Kennewick Man:

5. Zheng He:

6. Ferdinand Magellan:

7. Hernando de Soto:

8. Martin Luther:

9. French Huguenots:

10. Henry VII (England):

11. Francisco Pizarro:

12. Jacques Cartier:

13. John Calvin:

14. Sir Francis Drake:

15. Sir Walter Raleigh:

16. Roanoke:

17. *The Devastation of the Indies:*

18.   Hispaniola:

19.   Marco Polo:

20.   Mayans:

Multiple Choice Questions:

1.   The first people to settle in the Americas came from
     A.   Europe.
     B.   Asia.
     C.   South America.
     D.   North Africa.
     E.   Russia.
     Page Reference: 6

2.   All of the following were Mesoamerican civilizations EXCEPT
     A.   Incas.
     B.   Aztecs.
     C.   Mayans.
     D.   all of the above.
     E.   None of the above.
     Page Reference: 10

3.   Around A.D. 1000, the Vikings explored
     A.   Iceland.
     B.   Greenland.
     C.   Denmark.
     D.   Vinland.
     E.   Ireland.
     Page Reference: 15

4.   In the early fifteenth century, China was
     A.   visited by Marco Polo.
     B.   defeated by the French under Jacque Cartier.
     C.   victorious over England's Royal Navy.
     D.   crushed by Japan at the Battle of Bejing.
     E.   a major sea power led by Admiral Zheng He.
     Page Reference: 15

5. In 1492, King Ferdinand and Queen Isabella of Spain
    A.   sponsored Christopher Columbus's voyage.
    B.   drove Islam from their realm.
    C.   forced Jews into exile.
    D.   All of the above.
    E.   None of the above.
    Page Reference: 18

6. The Spanish arrived in the West Indies and they
    A.   enslaved many native peoples.
    B.   killed many Taino Indians and Caribs.
    C.   brought diseases that ravaged countless villages.
    D.   All of the above.
    E.   None of the above.
    Page Reference: 24

7. One reason Cortés was able to conquer the Aztec Empire is because
    A.   Indians were eager to convert to Roman Catholicism.
    B.   of Spain's alliance with the Inca Empire.
    C.   coastal Indians oppressed by the Aztecs became willing allies of the Spanish.
    D.   the Spanish had so many soldiers.
    E.   of their alliance with France.
    Page Reference: 26

8. Pizarro was able to conquer the Incas in part because
    A.   of his French military skill.
    B.   smallpox killed many Incas.
    C.   he had such a large troop of soldiers.
    D.   the Spanish came in peace.
    E.   of the failure of their Mayan allies to send help in time.
    Page Reference: 27

9. Henry VIII of England was the monarch who
    A.   built a sizable navy during his reign.
    B.   fought with France over Brazil.
    C.   converted his nation to Lutheranism.
    D.   returned England to Roman Catholic belief.
    E.   opposed all overseas adventures.
    Page Reference: 34

10. Against the Aztecs, the Spanish were fortunate that
    A.   laboring under heavy Aztec taxes, the coast peoples became their allies.
    B.   they were smarter than the Aztecs.
    C.   Spain had long used hit and run tactics in warfare.
    D.   the Aztecs were outnumbered by the Spanish.
    E.   they were braver than the natives.
    Page Reference: 26

11. The voyage of Ferdinand Magellan
    A. began in the seventeenth century.
    B. actually included Tsarist Russia.
    C. revealed the vast width of the Pacific.
    D. was based on the slave trade.
    E. failed to reach Mexico first in Magellan's race with Cortez
    Page Reference: 25

12. The Pope divided the Americas between Spain and
    A. France.
    B. Italy.
    C. Portugal.
    D. England.
    E. The Netherlands.
    Page Reference: 19

13. In the sixteenth century when English textile exports fell,
    A. this helped the nation by reducing inflation.
    B. the navy no longer had the money to continue costly overseas adventures.
    C. this encouraged slave rebellions against the Spanish.
    D. increased overseas expansion was partly due to the search for new markets.
    E. the cloth industry became dominated by Spain.
    Page Reference: 35

14. The Columbian Exchange of the last 500 years
    A. actually began in the nineteenth century.
    B. was a dramatic swapping of organisms between once-isolated continents.
    C. refers to the price that gold from the Americas brought back in Europe.
    D. was originally only between Spain and France.
    E. matters really only in terms of religion.
    Page Reference: 21

15. Sir Francis Drake on a voyage to the Pacific was able to
    A. circumnavigate the Caribbean.
    B. claim California for England as "new Albion."
    C. visit what is today Canada.
    D. alienate his royal support in London by his attacks on the Spanish.
    E. occupy a large part of India.
    Page Reference: 35

MAP QUESTION:

After looking at Map 1.4 discuss the penetration of the Europeans into North America in the sixteenth century. What explains why they went to certain places and avoided others?

CONNECTING HISTORY

Explain how people developed ways to discover where they were when on the open sea. How have new inventions changed sea travel?

INTERPRETING HISTORY

Explain how you think it would have felt to be a European hearing the Aztec defense of their gods. What is the basis of the Aztec argument?

ENVISIONING HISTORY

How would you explain that Europeans had such difficulty in changing their maps to fit the new evidence provided by people like Marco Polo and Magellan?

THE WIDER WORLD

Discuss how innovation passes between different peoples as you explain the importance of the change from the square sail to the lateen sail.

Answers to Multiple Choice Questions

1.	B		9.	A
2.	A		10.	A
3.	D		11.	C
4.	E		12.	C
5.	D		13.	D
6.	D		14.	B
7.	C		15.	B
8.	B			

Chapter 2
European Footholds on the Fringes of North America,
1600–1660

Learning Objectives:

After reading Chapter 2, you should be able to:

1. Discuss early Spanish incursions into the New World through the use of missions and forts.
2. Understand the aims of early Spanish explorers and how they encountered competition from the French and the Dutch.
3. Explain the motivations behind England's exploration of the Atlantic coast.
4. Describe the various Spanish, French, Dutch, and English settlements and understand some of the difficulties and successes encountered.
5. Discuss European and Native American contacts throughout this period.
6. Understand the Puritan Experiment and its aims.
7. Describe the Massachusetts Bay and Virginia Companies.
8. Discuss the unique character of the Maryland colony.

Time Line

1580
Spain's King Philip II claimed the throne of Portugal as his own, thus uniting the two great seafaring countries

1602
Dutch East India Company established

1606
Virginia Company chartered by James I

1607
Philip commanded an outpost be created on the coast of California as a way-station for Spanish galleons crossing the Pacific from the Philippines

1608
Samuel de Champlain established the outpost of Quebec in a narrow strait of the St. Lawrence River

1610
Henry Hudson, working for the English crown, explored the strait and bay in northern Canada that still bears his name

1624
King James annulled the Virginia Company's charter, creating in its stead a royal colony

1632
George Calvert granted 10 million acres of land adjacent to Virginia by Charles I to establish the royal colony of Maryland

1660
All four great European naval powers (Spain, France, Holland, and England) had established lasting footholds on the coast of the new continent

Chapter Overview

Envious of Spain's wealth, other European countries were soon competing for colonial spoils. This chapter looks at French, Dutch, and English programs for colonization in North America, as well as the motivations of the colonists in New England and the Chesapeake colonies.

I. Spain's Ocean-Spanning Reach

A. Vizcaino in California and Japan

Spain's imperial objectives included global markets in the East. Instructions from the Crown ordered the viceroy to create a Spanish settlement at Monterey Bay in California as a protective port for merchant ships returning from the Philippines and Japan.

The viceroy engaged Sebastian Vizcaino to do the job but soon after diverted needed funds to search for the fabled North Pacific islands of gold and silver. Vizcaino, powerless to complete the king's outpost, was soon directed to Japan in search of the legendary islands. He brought back to Spain a delegation of Japanese, but no gold. Spain's plans to colonize California were postponed.

B. Onate Creates a Spanish Foothold in the Southwest

While Spanish officials (peninsulares) debated over the wisdom of maintaining outposts like Fort Augustine, Florida, wealthy individuals like Juan de Onate secured permission from Mexican officials to establish a settlement in the northern Pueblo lands of New Mexico. He predicted New Mexico would outshine the rest of New Spain, but the native peoples, climate, and geography failed to cooperate with Onate's grand schemes. Brutal repression was necessary to secure aid from local villages, while settlers gave up and returned to central Mexico, convinced that nothing could grow in the harsh landscape. Onate's explorations did not find the Atlantic Ocean to the north or the Pacific Ocean within easy reach on the west. Franciscan friars converted several hundred Pueblo peoples, and pleaded with the Crown for the right to continue their harvest of souls in the region. Alerted to growing English and French interests in territories claimed by Spain, the Crown committed itself to maintaining the region but changed its governor. The small colony at the village of Santa Fe received news from central Mexico only once every three years. Unlike the French, Dutch, or English tradition of allotting citizenship, all townspeople were counted as Spanish citizens, whether Spanish, Mexican Indians, Africans, or mixed-race children (mestizos).

C. New Mexico Survives: New Flocks among Old Pueblos

The Spanish decision to retain and grow its settlements in New Mexico meant a reshaping of life for every ethnic type in the region. Missions proliferated, but converts were reluctant and few. Friars forbade traditional celebrations, destroyed sacred objects, and punished any backsliding severely. Soldiers from the presidios (forts) enforced these policies of the friars, as well as taxing local Pueblos for food, clothing, and servants. Despite these problems, Pueblo peoples found Spanish plants and animals useful and incorporated them into their lifestyle. Cattle were a problem, but horses, sheep, and donkeys were a benefit, as were plants such as wheat, onions, chilies, peas, peaches, plums, and cherries. Metal tools and axes improved cultivation, and wool became part of the rich spinning and weaving traditions of the Pueblo peoples.

D. Conversion and Rebellion in Spanish Florida

In Florida, Spanish cattle ranches were more successful than Spanish missions. Native population counts, assaulted by crushing diseases as well as corvee labor (required work hours on Spanish projects) and lack of food, began to plummet, and entire villages ceased to exist. Indian rebellions were quickly and firmly stamped out, with an eye to European competition for Spanish Florida. Epidemics of foreign diseases were unwittingly spread by both Friars and Indian bearers traveling into the interior.

II. France and Holland: Overseas Competition for Spain

A. The Founding of New France

England, Holland, and France secured islands and challenged Spanish control of the Caribbean. Having established a firm presence in the region, France concentrated on developing lands to the north in Canada. Their yearly fishing trips became even more lucrative with the realization that native peoples would trade beaver robes for cheap iron pots, with both parties feeling they received the best bargain. Explorations led to temporary settlements that had little lasting impact. However, Samuel de Champlain's use of his gun in support of his Algonquian neighbors' war against their Iroquois enemies produced a surprise victory and strong alliance with the Algonquians, as well as the lasting enmity of the Iroquois Confederation. By 1640, the French settlement had over 350 inhabitants and included 64 families, 116 women, 29 Jesuits and 53 soldiers.

B. Competing for the Beaver Trade

While the French expanded their influence on the fur trade throughout the northern extent of the Great Lakes, trading and arming the native populations with guns, Dutch fur traders founded Fort Orange on the Hudson River, trading with and arming the Iroquois League. Contagious disease and warfare—as always—took a dreadful toll, and resulted in a continuous round of "mourning wars" (a.k.a. Beaver Wars). Attempts by French Jesuit priests to convert the Indians finally settled on the four major villages of Huronia; they later moved their converts to praying missions close to French forts. By 1660, New France was thinly settled, weakly defended, and poorly supplied—its future was in doubt.

C. A Dutch Colony on the Hudson River

In 1608, the Dutch East India Company hired Henry Hudson, English-born navigator and arctic explorer, to attempt to locate a potential connecting waterway from the Atlantic to the Pacific. Confounded by snowstorms in Scandinavia, Hudson and his crew sailed down the American coast, visiting Chesapeake and Delaware Bays and New York harbor. Here, flying the Dutch flag, Hudson sailed up the river that still bears his name. Subsequent explorations claimed the land between the Delaware and Connecticut Rivers as New Amsterdam, to be administered by the new Dutch West India Company, created in 1621. The Company sponsored numerous settlements along the Connecticut and Delaware Rivers and the Atlantic coast. Dutch settlements successfully attracted colonizers and Crown support.

D. "All Sorts of Nationalities": Diverse New Amsterdam

The Dutch Colony of New Amsterdam quickly became the most cosmopolitan of European colonies in the Americas, with settlers from Holland, Belgium, Sweden, Finland, Switzerland, and England and religious convictions as diverse as Walloon Protestants, Quakers, and European Jews (who were segregated in a specific neighborhood called a ghetto). By 1664, African arrivals, granted "half-freedom" status, made up more than ten percent of New Netherlands's population, and at least half of them lived in Lower Manhattan.

III. English Beginnings on the Atlantic Coast

A. The Virginia Company and Jamestown

The failed Roanoke experiment warned individual investors that developing the wealth of America could be a costly venture. The next effort, chartered by James I in 1606, was the

Virginia Company on the Chesapeake Bay under the direction of a governor and council. The local Indian confederacy led by Powhatan chose an unequal diplomatic friendship, and the stronger "father" provided food and assistance to the weaker English "children," fostering expectations that the future would include mutually beneficial trade, as it had for tribes dealing with the French and Dutch. The Jamestown settlers included a large number of gentlemen unused to physical labor; they had expected immediate riches and found none.

B. "Starving Time" and Seeds of Representative Government

When hard work and starvation ensued, only the arrival of additional settlers kept the colony alive. Even so, they had to rely heavily on the native population for food. Unable to find readily exploitable precious metals, the quest to find a stable and profitable cash crop began. It took a decade to refine West Indian tobacco plants into an exportable crop. With labor, rather than land, at a premium, the majority of workers were English indentured servants, attracted by the promise of sizeable acreage at the end of their contract period. The high cost of African slaves meant that they would only gradually become key elements of the successful tobacco plantation society.

C. Launching the Plymouth Colony

To gather capital and labor, the Virginia Company began distributing legal charters to various groups to erect towns for settlement and cultivation. Between 1619 and 1623, the company granted more than 40 of these charters. Two such charters came to the ownership of members within a band of English Protestants exiled to Holland for religious differences with the king. One of these groups of separatists set sail from Plymouth in 1620 on the *Mayflower*. Storms and faulty navigation caused the settlers to make landfall at Cape Cod in modern-day Massachusetts.

IV. The Puritan Experiment

A. Formation of the Massachusetts Bay Company

In the northeast, religiously motivated settlements began at Plymouth and Massachusetts Bay. At Plymouth, the Pilgrims developed a small farming community, depending on the charity of the Wampanoag tribe led by Massasoit. In 1629, the Massachusetts Bay area became the site of a better-organized settlement of English Puritans who, under a new charter, sought to create a social experiment called the Massachusetts Bay Company. Their aim was to show the English an example of how to be piously religious as well as financially successful.

B. "We Shall Be As a City upon a Hill"

Over the next decade, 70,000 people left England for America. Many sailed to the West Indies, but a large contingent of Puritans arrived in the Massachusetts Bay Colony, enlarging the population and providing more labor to turn out the basic needs for survival. They brought with them the Calvinist ideals that embodied their religion and work ethic. These earlier settlers traded food, lodging, and raw building materials to the newest arrivals in return for textiles, tools, money, and labor. By 1640, English settlements had sprung up along the coast and up the Connecticut River where earlier smallpox infestations had removed the native menace. This rapid expansion put a quick strain on limited resources and caused church fathers to impose civic order.

C. Dissenters: Roger Williams and Ann Hutchinson

The Puritans were self-appointed saints, and as such believed God had chosen them for a special mission in this world. Not everyone, however, believed in the idea that a mandate from God required dominance of the Indians or subjugation of women by men. Roger Williams, a new arrival in the Boston area of the Massachusetts Bay Colony, angered local clerics with his views on separation of church and state and the invalidity of the king's land grants. Williams felt that Native Americans had the only right to sell land to the Puritans. Unwilling to listen, angry magistrates banished Williams from Massachusetts. He moved south and set up a township for other dissenters called Providence and sometime later sailed back to England to secure his own charter for the colony of Rhode Island.

Ann Hutchinson, an English native, had a vision of God telling her to follow her long-time minister to the New World. She did so in 1634, migrating to Boston with husband and 15 children. Soon after, she began hosting religious discussions in her home, which troubled the authorities. Accused of anarchy and dangerous anti-Puritan ideas about the nature of divine forgiveness, she and her growing number of followers were labeled Antinomians. Hutchinson herself was convicted of contempt and sedition in a two-day hearing and forced into exile. She moved first to Williams's Rhode Island and then to the Hudson Valley, where she and most of her family were killed by Indians.

D. Expansion and Violence: The Pequot War

Increasing power among Puritans in England resulted in an English Civil War that overthrew the monarchy and established in its place the English Commonwealth. In America, expanding Puritan settlements provoked a war with the Pequot tribe living along the Connecticut River. Fearing Pequot intentions, the Massachusetts Bay Colony recruited Narragansett and Mohegan Indians and waged a war so brutal that the Indian allies were shocked at the destruction and slaughter. The Mystic village massacre served as an effective threat to neighboring tribes, who reluctantly ceded lands to the English settlers.

V. The Chesapeake Bay Colonies

The successful tobacco experiment meant increasing tensions with the Powhatan Confederacy, as land-hungry Englishmen began to seize corn supplies and burn villages thought to harbor English runaways. Their aim was to convince the Indians to abide by English laws.

A. The Demise of the Virginia Company

The arrival of 3,500 additional settlers created so much tension that the remnants of the Powhatan Confederacy finally retaliated with a ten-year war that almost destroyed the Chesapeake colonies. In London, tales of the disaster fanned the flames of opposition to the Virginia Company, leading King James to annul the company's charter in 1624, making Virginia a royal colony controlled and taxed by the Crown. Barely surviving and rebuilding with newly arriving Englishmen, the colony of Virginia once again grew to become a major force in the area. A second major Indian war, begun a decade later, resulted in the defeat of the Indian Confederacy. Land-hungry colonists swarmed into territory once held by the tribes.

B. Maryland: The Catholic Refuge

The second colony that emerged in the Chesapeake Bay area, Maryland, began in 1634 as a Catholic haven with laws protecting freedom of religion. Within 15 years, the majority of Protestants who moved to the colony took control and repealed these laws. In Maryland, as in the northern colonies, strong religious conviction did not result in respect for the religious convictions of others, but by 1660, with the reestablishment of the English monarchy, tolerance returned to the colony.

C. The Dwellings of English Newcomers

Virginia and Maryland had perhaps 35,000 settlers by 1660, while New England contained maybe 25,000. From the start, housing was a prime concern. Different climates led to contrasting architectural styles. In New England, harsher weather and longer winters caused houses to be larger, with a central fireplace. Early Chesapeake houses were less solid and smaller, with a dirt or plank floor.

D. The Lure of Tobacco

After a series of failed export products, Chesapeake residents hit upon the cultivation of tobacco. Virginia's export of the weed grew from 2,000 pounds in 1615 to 500,000 pounds by 1626. In 1620, the British government gave Bermuda and Virginia a near monopoly on tobacco production. Even when prices were low, tobacco remained the lifeblood of the region.

Identification

Explain the significance of each of the following:

1.   Mayflower:

2.   Sebastian Vizcaino:

3.   Tokugawa Dynasty:

4.   Straits of Anian:

5.   Juan de Onate:

6.   Franciscans:

7.   Florida:

8.   Dutch East India Company:

9.   Samuel de Champlain:

10. Cardinal Richelieu:

11. Ignatius Loyola:

12. The Beaver Wars:

13. Henry Hudson:

14. New Netherland:

15. Waloons:

16. Peter Stuyvesant:

17. "half-freedom":

18. enclosure movement:

19. The Virginia Company:

20. Powhatan:

21. Tobacco:

22. The Massachusetts Bay Company:

23. Puritanism:

24. Roger Williams:

25. Anne Hutchinson:

26. The Pequot War:

27. Opechancanough:

28. George Calvert:

29. Maryland:

30. Anne Bradstreet:

Multiple Choice Questions:

1. When the Pilgrims landed at Plymouth in 1620, the English-speaking Indian they
   encountered was
   A. Leif Erikson.
   B. Tecumseh.
   C. Tonto.
   D. Squanto.
   E. Metacom.
   Page Reference: 40

2. In 1580, in order to consolidate his power, Spain's Philip II laid claim to the throne of
   A. Holland.
   B. Spain.
   C. England.
   D. Sweden.
   E. Portugal.
   Page Reference: 40

3. In 1611, Sebastian Vizcaino began a search for islands fabled for their
   A. silk.
   B. furs.
   C. gold and silver.
   D. spices.
   E. fountain of youth.
   Page Reference: 41

4. By 1660, England had established a colonial foothold in the Caribbean at
   A. Trinidad.
   B. St. Maarten.
   C. St. Lucia.
   D. Barbados.
   E. Haiti.
   Page Reference: 47

5. In 1608, French leader Champlain established the outpost of
   A. Tordesillas.
   B. Quebec.
   C. Toronto.
   D. Westphalia.
   E. Versailles.
   Page Reference: 49

6. The Dutch commander who seized New Sweden was
   A. Samuel de Champlain.
   B. Peter Minuit.
   C. Ronald Van Raak.
   D. Peter Stuyvestant.
   E. John Cabot.
   Page Reference: 53

7. The English leader who chartered the Virginia company in 1606 was
   A. Queen Elizabeth I.
   B. John Winthrop.
   C. John Locke.
   D. Sir Francis Drake
   E. James I
   Page Reference: 54

8. The Virginia colony was a financial disaster until the introduction of
    A.   yams.
    B.   indigo.
    C.   tobacco.
    D.   cotton.
    E.   oranges.
    Page Reference: 56

9. The leader of the Massachusetts Bay Colony was the Puritan
    A.   John Winthrop.
    B.   Thomas Hooker.
    C.   Roger Williams.
    D.   William Bradford.
    E.   Lord Baltimore.
    Page Reference: 59

10. Immigration to New England slowed during the 1640s because of
    A.   the Spanish invasion.
    B.   religious and political upheaval at home.
    C.   pressure from French America to the north.
    D.   War with the Dutch over New Amsterdam.
    E.   a major uprising by the local native Americans.
    Page Reference: 63

MAP QUESTION:

Examine the hand-drawn maps of North America provided in the second chapter. How would these primitive maps, which inaccurately show land areas, affect exploration or settlement?

CONNECTING HISTORY

Some people conjecture that space colonization may be in the near future. Under what circumstances do you think this could be successful? Who would go?

INTERPRETING HISTORY

Why was Anne Bradstreet an unusual poet for the times?

ENVISIONING HISTORY

Why would people, like Jefferson attack Chesapeake Housing? Do you agree or disagree with his argument?

THE WIDER WORLD

Explain how the argument for freedom of the seas was an attack on some seagoing nations and a defense of others? Which side do you agree with? Why?

Answers to Multiple Choice Questions

1. D
2. E
3. C
4. D
5. B
6. D
7. E
8. C
9. A
10. B

Chapter 3
Controlling the Edges of the Continent,
1660–1715

Learning Objectives:

After reading Chapter 3, you should be able to:

1. Discuss France's dominant role in exploring the new American continent.
2. Understand the ongoing expansion of Spanish settlements.
3. Discuss how the restoration of the English monarchy changed the nature of English expansion in the New World.
4. Discuss the English colonies and the colonists' relationship to Native Americans.
5. Explain how the Glorious Revolution in Europe affected the English colonies.
6. Understand the consequences of war and growth, financially and socially.
7. Outline the Salem, Massachusetts witch trials.

Time Line

1660
English monarchy restored in the guise of Charles II
Parliament passed Navigation Act designed to promote and protect English shipping and trade with the colonies

1661
King Louis XIV assumed personal control of the French nation at age 22

1664
Charles II seized Dutch colony of New Netherlands and its capitol New Amsterdam, renamed New York

1673
Louis Joliet and Jacques Marquette explored upper Mississippi River and deduce its path to the Gulf of Mexico

1675
Metacom's War began, also known as King Philip's War

1679
Charles II made New Hampshire a proprietorship

1680
Pueblo Revolt in New Mexico

1681
Charles II granted charter for Pennsylvania to Quaker aristocrat William Penn
Charles dissolved Parliament, angered by interference over line of royal succession

1682
La Salle led a contingent of French and Indians south from the Great Lakes to explore the lower Mississippi River; confirmed river path to the Gulf

1685
James II became King of England
Louis XIV revoked Edict of Nantes, stripping French Protestants of their legal rights

1688-1689
Glorious Revolution in England, abdication of James II, ascension of William and Mary to new limited monarchy

1689
King William's War, also known as the French and Indian War, erupted near Montreal; lasted eight years

1691
New Massachusetts charter granted, joining Plymouth settlement and Maine into Massachusetts Bay colony

1692
Salem Witch Trials

1699
Colony in French Louisiana

1700
Louis XIV maneuvered his own grandson onto the Spanish throne to become Philip V

1701
War of Spanish Succession began
English Parliament passed Act of Settlement detailing succession upon death of William (1702)

1715
Louis XIV died

1718
Earliest Spanish mission established in present-day Texas at San Antonio

Chapter Overview

European powers were quick to push into the North American interior, exploring the region, pressing their own claims to the empire, and putting pressure on the Spanish. This competition inevitably led to bloodshed as North America became the scene of a number of bloody proxy wars. The last of these, the Yamasee War in the South, ended Native American militancy in the section.

I. France and the American Interior

A. The Rise of the Sun King

The French king, Louis XIV, assumed command of the nation in 1661 at the age of 22. Living and ruling for 55 more years, Louis became a fixture in the political and religious spheres of Europe. He built monuments, dazzled the French nobility into complacency, and challenged the supremacy of the pope while centralizing his country's power as never before.

An adherent of the fiscal policy of mercantilism, Louis followed a path of economic self-sufficiency by avoiding foreign debt and amassing precious metals from French colonies abroad. Efficient use of labor resources and an aggressive trade policy generated much revenue and allowed Louis to finance huge building projects and wars.

In contrast to England, Louis declined to use France's overseas colonies as havens for religious dissidents and social outcasts. These dissidents were later compelled to seek refuge in the English colonies.

B. Exploring the Mississippi Valley

The French government followed a two-pronged approach to settlement in New France. Exploration was encouraged to expand French claims to American territory.

Adapting Indian canoes, the French explorer La Salle traversed westward to the Great Lakes and southward on the newly discovered Mississippi River to the Gulf of Mexico. LaSalle then claimed all the land drained by the river for France, proclaiming it Louisiana. French forts were networked at distant points to aid in the fur trade and provide logistical support for further exploration.

Settlement was encouraged to diversify economic growth, although small townships and farming communities grew slowly due to climate and living conditions. Concerned about depopulating France to build the colonies, the Crown decreased its support for major settlements in New France.

C. King William's War in the Northeast

Religion and economic competition fueled the French and English rivalry in Europe, finally boiling over into the American colonies in 1689. In that year, the Iroquois, equipped by the English, launched raids on the encroaching French near Montreal. The French, spread thin from administering the widening fur trade, nevertheless successfully used their native allies in an eight-year war of European empires, inflicting heavy damage on the Iroquois Confederation, as well as scattered English villages, farms, and frontier settlements.

At the conclusion of King William's War (also known as the French and Indian War), the Iroquois determined to remain neutral in any future confrontations between the two European powers. The European portion of the war ended in a stalemate where each belligerent returned the territory gained from the enemy. In America, this meant a strengthened position for the French with a long-time enemy subdued, and the freedom to expand forts and establish settlements along the length of the Mississippi River.

D. Founding the Louisiana Colony

Before the eruption of war in Europe in 1701, King Louis XIV took active steps to insure the control of its claims in the Gulf of Mexico and established defenses against the naval power of the Spanish. Repelling English explorers, an early French expedition founded the first Gulf fort at Biloxi Bay in 1699.

Subsequent French expeditions established a defensive base at Mobile and began to drive inland, up the course of the Mississippi, where a series of outposts began to thrive. Reinforcing the territorial claims of France, these outposts eventually stretched the length of the river and offered increased trade and protection to the native populations, thereby gaining their loyalty.

In 1712, the French government, depleted from a decade of warfare in Europe, granted control of Louisiana to a powerful Parisian merchant, Antoine Crozat, who resolved to make the colony profitable.

In 1715, the Louisiana population was approximately 300, but the French had established a solid claim on the interior of the American continent until the era of Napoleon and Thomas Jefferson, almost a century later.

II. The Spanish Empire on the Defensive

A. The Pueblo Revolt in New Mexico

Mismanagement fueled Indian rebellions throughout northern New Spain. Local administration proved to be corrupt, and effective communication with Spain was naturally slow, giving these local bureaucrats an unlimited potential to abuse the native populations.

The successful Pueblo Revolt of 1680 had the longest-lasting impact on Spanish policy. Drought, Apache and Navajo raids in response to Mexican slave raiders, the inability of the Spanish officials to protect villages from these raids, and religious issues were only a few of the long-standing grievances of the Pueblo people. When frustrated priests resorted to hanging, whipping, and selling "idolaters" into slavery, the villagers united around the charismatic San Juan Pueblo leader, Pope, and successfully defeated the military garrison and drove the remaining Spanish citizens from the region. The unusual coalition of independent villages soon disintegrated over differences concerning leadership and objectives. When Spain regained control of the region, the Crown ordered fairer government, which included respect for Indian traditions. The Crown was more interested in maintaining control over the region than in purifying Indian souls.

B. Navajos and Spanish on the Southwestern Frontier

Among the repercussions of the Pueblo Revolt and fears of Spanish military reprisal was the dispersion of Pueblo peoples to Navajo villages, along with flocks of sheep, horses, and agricultural seeds. In their matriarchal society, Navajo women controlled the flocks and incorporated wool into their traditional cotton-weaving routine. Horses increased Navajo mobility and also entered the trade network, eventually reaching the Southern and Northern Plains, thus drastically altering Plains lifestyles and tribal relationships.

The Pueblo Revolt also brought repercussions for the Spanish, who realized their weakened and isolated position in the Southwest. Despite limited resources, administrators in Mexico City sent a few missionaries northward to spread Christianity and subdue native tribes. These missionaries, seeking to expand their nation's geographical knowledge, pushed into present-day Arizona and the Sonoran Desert by the 1690s.

C. Borderland Conflict in Texas and Florida

Earlier border conflicts with the French caused the Spanish to assert their claims and establish missions and forts in the area of Texas, named after the local Tejas Indians. Starting with San Antonio, the Spanish network expanded along the border between Louisiana and Texas and along the San Antonio River.

Indian resentment also grew in Florida, where demands for food and labor combined with the demands of the new religion and deadly diseases led to the deterioration of village lifestyle and tradition. As in other areas in New Spain, Crown laws concerning Indian legal rights and labor responsibilities were ignored. Rather than respecting unfenced Indian gardens, cattle roamed freely, and Indians who killed the cattle faced four months of servitude and the loss of their ears.

The new English colonies to the north gave Florida tribes the chance to ignore Spain and deal with a new English market in the deerskin trade. Each country tried to force exclusive tribal loyalty. Caught in the middle of Spanish and English imperial aspirations, Florida tribes dealt with harsh military action from the Spanish and slave raids from Carolina.

III. England's American Empire Takes Shape

A. Monarchy Restored and Navigation Controlled

As France's Louis XIV ascended to his throne, England underwent a radical change in government that changed how English colonists lived. In the 1640s, during a bloody civil war, English citizens supporting Puritan freedom of religion and Parliament-based rule overthrew the reigning Stuart family, beheaded Charles I, and put an end to the hereditary monarchy.

For the brief years that followed, England became a republican commonwealth, ruled by the Lord Protector of Parliament, Oliver Cromwell. His death in 1658 caused members of government to reconsider reestablishing the monarchy. Two years later, the English government invited Charles's son back from exile and restored him to the throne as Charles II.

After nullifying all government decrees from the late Cromwell, Charles II moved quickly to revenge his father. Those responsible parties that could not escape to Puritan New England were summarily executed. The American colonies continued to grow with the influx of political dissidents. Sea trade flourished as a result of population increase and close proximity of the majority of people to a shoreline. Increased merchant shipping traffic prompted the need for regulation to safeguard colonial interests.

In 1660, Parliament passed the Navigation Act, designed to promote British seaborne trade through regulation regarding who could carry which products. Foreign-owned ships were not allowed to transport colonial goods, key non-English products from the colonies had to be shipped on British transports, and a list of luxury items produced overseas—enumerated articles—could no longer be sent to England via a foreign port.

The Navigation Acts (several more followed the original) fueled shipbuilding in the tree-rich New World. Britain's navy and merchant fleet grew tremendously as colonial trade became a main staple of the English economy.

B. Fierce Anglo-Dutch Competition

English and Dutch trade rivalries also affected the colonies. The Navigation Acts had cut deeply into the Dutch share of colonial trade and prompted a decade of renewed warfare with the British. These Anglo-Dutch skirmishes usually ended in stalemate, but the subsequent Treaty of Westminster in 1674 granted England valuable rights in Africa and advantages in the growing slave trade as well as seizure of the poorly defended Dutch colony of New Netherland and its capital of New Amsterdam.

These Dutch holdings had long been disputed by Britain, who claimed the renamed New York area as part of its original rights in the continent. The naval fleet that arrived to back up the English claim was unnecessary, as the Dutch governor surrendered the colony without a fight. The enthusiasm of Dutch colonists waned under an appointed governor and council whose decisions were unrestrained by local opinion. Arriving English settlers also resented the lack of representation and lobbied successfully to acquire it. However, their first action, approving government by consent of the governed, angered the Duke of York, who ordered it disbanded.

Despite their loss, the Dutch continued to be a presence in the colony and eventually integrated themselves into the local society.

C. The New Restoration Colonies

The restoration to monarchal rule also resulted in the establishment of new colonies as proprietorships, opening Carolina, New Hampshire, New Jersey, and Pennsylvania. Carolina quickly prospered using slavery to develop plantations that supplied rice to Barbados and its fellow slave regions and indigo (deep blue dye) to the British textile industry. Pennsylvania prospered by supplying foodstuffs and various craft goods, especially chains and metal tools, to the existing colonies to the north and south, and in the West Indies.

D. The Contrasting Worlds of Pennsylvania and Carolina

In 1682, William Penn established Philadelphia as the capital of Pennsylvania and within two decades it had more than 2,000 residents. Penn, a devout Quaker and pacifist, dealt fairly with the Lenni-Lenape Indians and practiced religious toleration. From the start, Pennsylvania was diverse and in 1701, Penn agreed to a unicameral legislature with full legal power.

By contrast, Anthony Ashley-Cooper wished to establish a stable aristocratic system based upon a clearly stratified society. Moreover, Carolina was based on racial slavery, which is not surprising given the proprietors' interest in England's slave-trading monopoly in Africa.

IV. Bloodshed in the English Colonies: 1670–1690

A. Metacom's War in New England

By 1675, the Native Americans of the Atlantic coastal region had lived through several decades of colonization by Europeans. Disagreements flourished about how much European culture should be assimilated. Many Native Americans spoke English to enhance trade relations and some had aspired to traditional higher education. Massasoit, the Wampanoag leader who had befriended the Pilgrims, was careful to ensure that his two sons, Wamsutta and Metacom, were schooled in English ways. Wamsutta died in the 1660s and Metacom (now called King Philip, having succeeded both his father and brother) suspected a sinister plot by the British.

Metacom held his tongue over the next decade as his resentment grew. He saw his people abused and cheated by the colonists and watched the white population grow. Open hostilities erupted in 1675 when three Wampanoags were executed as murderers of another Wampanoag informant, an informant who had learned of Metacom's anger and plans for revenge.

In the summer and fall, Metacom's braves raided town after town along the Connecticut River, gathering new recruits as they traveled. United colonists surprised and overwhelmed a main band of rebel natives, burning them in their hastily prepared defenses. Some escaped this "Great Swamp Fight," but the death toll stood at about 600 Wampanoags and other tribesmen.

Infuriated, the neighboring Narragansett tribe joined forces with Metacom and his growing cadre of natives. Ultimately, sickness, hunger, and clashes with pro-European tribes broke the Metacom coalition; he was taken prisoner and beheaded.

B. Bacon's Rebellion in Virginia

In Virginia, the grievances of 6,000 indentured Europeans and 2,000 black slaves combined with frontier tensions in a bloody rebellion led by Nathaniel Bacon. Governor Berkeley was not successful in controlling the rebellion, which grew with the addition of poor land owners and runaway servants.

In an attempt to demonstrate support for his policies, Berkeley held the first election in 14 years, but Bacon's followers dominated the new Assembly, which passed laws returning the vote to landless men, and reduced much of the corruption that had crept into Virginia's governance under Berkeley.

Bacon's followers destroyed Indian villages on the frontier, and Jamestown on the coast. The rebellion evaporated with the death of Bacon and the arrival of English troops. On the frontier, Indian anger against settlers increased, while the small group of Virginia gentry moved to erect barriers between black and white servants.

C. The "Glorious Revolution" in England

In 1678, rumors began to circulate in England that the Catholics were plotting to kill the Protestant king Charles II so that a Catholic, his brother James, could take power. Parliament, fearful of rule by a Catholic, declared that James should be removed from the natural line of succession. Parliament argued that a better choice for ruler would be one of James's daughters from his first marriage—most specifically Mary, who had just married her Dutch Cousin, William of Orange.

Angered by the debate on succession, Charles disbanded Parliament in 1681 and ruled alone for the remaining four years of his life. When he died without Parliament's oversight, his natural successor, James II, ascended the throne in 1685.

Fear and suspicion of Catholics escalated in the people of England when James also dissolved Parliament, created a standing army, and placed a Catholic in command of the English Navy. Soon after, James's queen gave birth to a male heir, ushering in a new dynasty of Catholic rulers.

United by their fear, England's political class appealed to Protestant William of Orange to lead an army from Holland and seize the English crown. William did this in 1688, staging a bloodless invasion of the island country. James abdicated and fled into exile. William and his wife, James's daughter Mary, were proclaimed joint monarchs of the Glorious Revolution. They accepted a Bill of Rights from Parliament and handed over most of the sovereign's traditional powers.

D. The "Glorious Revolution" in America

In America, James's creation of the Dominion of New England met fierce resistance, which increased under the heavy-handed governance of Edmond Andros. James II finally abdicated and fled the country. Crowned king, William accepted English demands for a bill of rights, greater freedom of the press, and freedom of religion for Protestant dissenters. Unlike James II, William supported Parliamentary power. As information about these conditions in England reached the colonies, colonists in Boston and New York removed the Dominion officials appointed by James II. Colonists in the Chesapeake also seized power from his appointees.

V. Consequences of War and Growth: 1690–1715

A. Salem's Wartime Witch Hunt

In 1692, an outbreak of witchcraft accusations occurred in Essex County, Massachusetts, near the Maine frontier. In the early 1600s, witchcraft trials were common in Europe, and in the colonies Christians had already prosecuted and executed several accused witches. Salem, however, was a special case with more than 200 accused witches.

Early in 1692, several young girls in Salem began to suffer violent fits, followed by vivid hallucinations. The girls accused a slave couple of Indian or African origin of bewitching them. By April, the girls had accused seven more people, who in turn accused others of the township.

Show trials in abundance followed, with public hangings of those hapless enough not to appear convincing. Only when prominent leaders of the church and community fell under accusation did the girls begin to recant. The colonial governor intervened, and emptied the jails.

B. The Uneven Costs of War

While war in America meant frightening raids for frontier settlements, there were those in coastal towns who profited from the war. The challenge of supplying troops with necessities combined with a growing trade in black market merchandise, created opportunity and wealth for a few and an expanded job market for others. Poor families suffered under increased taxes, higher food prices, and military pressures. While the rich prospered under the wartime economy, with 5 percent controlling 40 percent of the wealth, over 60 percent of the population controlled only 13 percent of the wealth.

C. Storm Clouds in the South

Increasing settlement in Carolina created new pressures on southern tribal lands and local resources. Tuscarora tribesmen, reacting to cheating traders and settler pressures, began war in 1711. Settlers combined with Yamasee warriors to crush the rebellion. Most of the remaining Tuscaroras moved north from their southern homelands and became the sixth nation in the Iroquois League. By 1715, settler pressure for Yamasee land again led to war. Yamasee and Creek Native Americans, Spanish settlers in Florida, and French traders in the Alabama territory joined in bringing war again to the English frontier.

Identification

Explain the significance of each of the following:

1. King Louis XIV:

2. The Edict of Nantes:

3. Louis Joliet:

4. Rene-Robert Cavelier, Sieur de La Salle:

5. Louisiana:

6. King William's War:

7. Monsieur Cadillac:

8. The Pueblo Revolt:

9. Eusebio Kino:

10. Unicameral legislature:

11. Oliver Cromwell:

12. The Navigation Acts:

13. The Peace of Westminster:

14. William Penn:

15. Wampanoags:

16. Metacom's War:

17. Massasoit:

18. Bacon's Rebellion:

19. The Glorious Revolution:

20. William of Orange:

21. Salem, Massachusetts:

22. The Act of Settlement:

23. The Naval Stores Act of 1705:

Multiple Choice Questions:

1. King Louis XIV was nicknamed the
   A. Ruthless.
   B. Father of Paris.
   C. Sun King.
   D. Conqueror.
   E. Great Communicator.
   Page Reference: 72

2. In 1682, La Salle claimed the lower Mississippi and the river basin Louisiana for
   A. Indians.
   B. debtors.
   C. Catholics.
   D. slaves.
   E. France.
   Page Reference: 74

3. The Wampanoag leader, Metacom, was also known as
   A. King Philip.
   B. Squanto.
   C. Pequot.
   D. Wamsutta.
   E. King William.
   Page Reference: 88

4. The authoritarian governor of Virginia whose heavy-handed actions touched off Bacon's Rebellion was
   A. Thomas Hutchinson.
   B. Charles Ashley-Smith.
   C. William Pitt.
   D. Nathanial Bacon.
   E. Sir William Berkeley.
   Page Reference: 89

5. In the Glorious Revolution of 1689, William of Orange intervened in English politics to depose
   A. Charles I.
   B. Edmond Andros.
   C. Elizabeth I.
   D. James II.
   E. Charles II
   Page Reference: 91

6. In 1692, an outburst of witchcraft accusations engulfed
   A. Boston.
   B. Salem Village.
   C. Louis Joliet and other French Catholics.
   D. New York City.
   E. all the English North American colonies.
   Page Reference: 94

7. The Indian leader of the Pueblo Rebellion of 1680 was
   A. Diego de Vargas.
   B. Juan de Onate.
   C. Pope.
   D. Pedro Naranjo.
   E. Squanto.
   Page Reference: 79

8. When James, Duke of York, seized New Amsterdam from the Dutch, he renamed the colony
   A. New Boston.
   B. New Caledonia.
   C. Baltimore.
   D. New York.
   E. New London.
   Page Reference: 84

9. Nathanial Bacon drew support for his Virginia rebellion from
   A. the wealthy members of the Carolina colony.
   B. the Scottish Highlands.
   C. Indian tribes.
   D. neighboring Georgia gentry.
   E. indentured Europeans and enslaved Africans.
   Page Reference: 89

10. To King James II's opponents, it seemed he wished to establish
    A. a new Carolina colony.
    B. Catholic rule and a Catholic dynasty.
    C. a return to Puritan values in the colonies.
    D. a joint monarchy with William of Orange.
    E. All of the above.
    Page Reference: 91

MAP QUESTION:

Examine the maps in this chapter. According to European convention, exploration of an area more firmly establishes a country's claim to a region. The existence of colonies confirms the claims. By studying the maps, what can you conclude about European activity between 1660 and 1715? Regardless of international understandings, who had control of the land claimed by Spain, England, or France?

CONNECTING HISTORY

In the case of a national tragedy such as the terrorist attacks of September 11, 2001, should a person come under suspicion solely on the basis of identification with a particular nationality, religion, or ethnic group?

INTERPRETING HISTORY

Given the enormous negative influence that European colonization had on the Native Americans, would any amount of sympathy regarding their plight from colonial leaders of the times have made a difference in the resulting actions of people like Metacom?

ENVISIONING HISTORY

Why don't we usually know as much about French colonial failures as we do about those of the British? What does this tell us about our own culture?

THE WIDER WORLD

Explain the different world views that led to distrust between French priests and Native Americans?

Answers to Multiple Choice Questions

1. C
2. E
3. A
4. E
5. D
6. B
7. C
8. D
9. E
10. B

Chapter 4
African Enslavement:
The Terrible Transformation

Learning Objectives:

After reading Chapter 4, you should be able to:

1. Understand the effect of the growing slave trade on the African tribes in terms of escalation of tribal warfare, slave raids, changes in tribal population, and culture.
2. Discuss the origins of the African slave trade and why it came to be.
3. Explain how the process of capture in Africa, the terrifying Atlantic journey, and torture were meant to produce a servile, industrious slave with no desire to rebel.
4. Appreciate the kinds of passive resistance demonstrated by African slaves in order to exert some measure of control over their lives.
5. Describe how interpersonal relationships and religion helped Africans endure the oppression of slavery.
6. Discuss how the slave trade developed in the Western Hemisphere.
7. Understand how constant fear of slave revolt prompted the white minority to create rigid systems of law to control every aspect of African labor.

Time Line

1565
African slave labor used to establish Spanish outpost at St. Augustine (Florida)

1625
Brazil led the Western Hemisphere in imported slaves and exported sugar

1640
Virginia passed law preventing blacks from bearing arms

1650
Slavery and sugar production growing quickly in English West Indies; few slaves in North American colonies

1652
Rhode Island colony passed statute limiting all involuntary servitude to no more than ten years

1662
Virginia General Assembly proclaimed that any child born of an Englishman and an African woman would be free or slave depending on the status of the mother; began a tradition of hereditary slavery

1665
Great Plague in England lowered population and created increased demand for alternative labor source

1676
Bacon's Rebellion in Virginia

1680
Virginia slave law created, spelled out punishments, including death for violent slaves

1691
Virginia statute created, condemning sexual mixing of Englishmen with other races; required freed slaves to be banished from the colony within six months of their release at the former master's expense; limited the parameters for granting freedom to slaves

1699
Thomas Bray established Society for Promoting Christian Knowledge; established Society for the Propagation of the Gospel in Foreign Parts (SPG) in 1701

1705
Virginia Negro Act allowed white indentured servants to sue their masters in court for mistreatment; blacks were not extended the same right

1732
Twenty-year charter for the new territory of Georgia granted to a group of English trustees; first group of settlers arrived in 1733

1735
Georgia proclaimed a free-white colony that prohibited slavery and refused to admit free blacks

1739
Stono Rebellion, largest slave uprising in colonial North America, near Charleston

1741
New York Slave Plot

1750
Free-white experiment in Georgia failed; law passed permitting slavery

1754
Some Considerations on the Keeping of Negroes published by the Quaker John Woolman
Georgia became royal colony

Chapter Overview

As the economic and social structure of the colonial world changed, so too did the institution of slavery. Demand grew and the institution increasingly defined itself racially. As profits increased, England entered the slave trade, and Africans, newly enslaved, struggled to make sense of this new, horrible world.

I. The Descent into Race Slavery

A. The Caribbean Precedent

As the need for fully controlled, inexpensive labor emerged in colonial expansion, Europeans devised religious and moral justifications for participation in the African slave trade. Spanish developers introduced black slavery to the Western Hemisphere, specifically in the Caribbean, as Indian populations declined due to disease and labor conditions. Agriculture and mining successes outgrew the ability of Spanish ships to deliver the required number of slaves, and the Spanish government actively sought shippers from the Dutch and other rival nations. Portugal, already delivering slaves to sugar colonies in the Azores, increased its activity in the lucrative slave trade to meet the new demand.

As Portugal developed Brazil, the slave trade naturally followed. Slavery also became the regional work force on English sugar plantations in Barbados. At the time of the earliest British colonies in America, black slaves, due to expense, were an insignificant portion of the labor force, which depended on white indentured labor.

B. Ominous Beginnings

Since the sixteenth century, African men had joined Spanish expeditions into the wilds of the Southeast; some had remained, starting families with natives. African slaves labored to build the Spanish outpost at St. Augustine in 1565. Africans did exist within the colonies of the French, Dutch, and English but not in great number. Most slaves at this time did not come from Africa but were second-generation African Americans from the Caribbean. There was no uniform code regarding the treatment of slaves, and experiences varied widely.

In the Massachusetts Bay area, early Puritan settlers in need of reliable labor began to import a few slaves from the Caribbean and even tried to negotiate a direct trade agreement with Africa. In 1652, Rhode Island passed a law restricting the length of involuntary servitude of any type to ten years.

In 1619, slaves were brought in number to Virginia. A series of Virginia statutes was created during the subsequent decades to systematically strip Africans of any rights and reduce them to mere property. Skin color became the distinguishing identifier of servitude. Throughout the 1640s and 1650s, planters in Virginia began to assume rights to the labor of Indians and Africans for life. Additionally, they claimed rights to any children produced by slave women of color.

C. Alternative Sources of Labor

Enslaved Native Americans were readily used but proved susceptible to European diseases and were harder to identify or capture when they ran away. Also, Indian wars to secure slaves tended to disrupt trade and increased the risks to villages, towns, and outlying farms in all of the colonies. Bacon's Rebellion and the Great Plague of London sounded a warning to colonial planters that indentured labor from Europe was not an inexhaustible resource. Moreover, abused and cheated indentured servants were quick to report their plight to potential indentures back in England; these potentials would simply book passage to another location.

In contrast, the African slaves had no avenue of redress for the mistreatments they encountered in the colonies and the Caribbean. Thus, no feedback or warnings made it back to Africa to deter relatives or tribesmen from falling into the same trap. Lack of communication perpetuated the Africans' plight.

D. The Fateful Transition

Although black slaves existed in British colonies, the growth of laws to support a slave system emerged gradually over the decades. Questions about the length of time one would be a slave, the status of slave children, and the legal restrictions regarding slave testimony were decided in colonial courts. Also struck down was the notion that the acceptance of Christianity could save an African from slavery; a Maryland law of 1664 closed that avenue of escape.

In approximately 20 years, English planters had conspired to transform black indentured servitude into hereditary slavery. African slaves, condemned to unpaid labor for life, had no method of complaint when they were punished for misdeeds, real or suggested. Therefore, they found themselves increasingly at the mercy of cruel masters sanctioned by the government to beat them into submission.

II. The Growth of Slave Labor Camps

A. Black Involvement in Bacon's Rebellion

Bacon's Rebellion, the major uprising that took place in the Chesapeake region in 1676, had a profound impact on Virginia's transition to racial slavery. The debacle saw Nathaniel Bacon and a group of aspiring Virginia gentry struggling against Indian groups of the frontier and an entrenched Jamestown oligarchy.

The rebellion underscored the need to find an alternative to the flow of predominately white indentured servants from England. Terms of service only lasted several years and freed servants were still young enough to become competitors to the masters. Those freed men, both black and white, made up the bulk of Bacon's following.

B. The Rise of a Slaveholding Tidewater Elite

The decision to use black slave labor in the Chesapeake region was based on the desire for profit and dependable long-term laborers. As better living conditions emerged, slaves could be expected to produce children, whose labor could also be exploited or who could be sold for a profit. Slave laborers worked long hours, at tasks specified by owners, and were moved without warning when their labor was desired elsewhere. These conditions were no better than convict labor camps. Africans would routinely be forced to work without pay for life and endure increasingly brutal physical punishment as motivation.

Slave ownership appealed to both the wealthy and those aspiring to wealth. Young white men, like William Byrd of Virginia, could earn enough money in business, purchase a few slaves for resale, and continue expanding their operations to gain wealth and power. Planters in Virginia increased their profits by expanding the head-right system, where 50 acres of land were provided for any person who brought a family member or worker into the colony, to include those who purchased slaves, thereby increasing their acreage as they increased the workforce.

C. Closing the Vicious Circle in the Chesapeake

The courts and the church also became influential in establishing the accepted conditions of slavery and white labor. Interracial ties became taboo; insistent couples were banished from the dominion. Blacks, regardless of their origins or status, were systematically stripped of any rights they might have thought they possessed.

White indentured servants retained the right to sue their masters for mistreatment according to the Negro Act of 1705, yet Africans had no such ability of judicial appeal. Masters who accidentally killed a slave during the course of inflicting punishment were held free of any felony. The system of government-approved enslaving of Africans was now firmly in place.

III. England Enters the Atlantic Slave Trade

England showed little initial interest in the slave trade, but profits from a growing sugar operation in Barbados quickly convinced Charles II of the slavery system's merits.

By 1670, the Crown granted a monopoly to the Royal African Company to exploit the African slave trade. The RAC kept up a steady flow of slave ships between Africa and the English colonies. Demand for slave labor, especially in the Caribbean, continued to drive the price of slaves higher. Greed compelled privateers to challenge the RAC monopoly, which ended officially in 1698. In 1713, English companies were contracted to supply African slaves to the Spanish colonies in America and continued to dominate the slave trade for the next three generations.

A. Trade Ties Between Europe and Africa

Dozens of European trading posts were set up all along the sub-Saharan coastline in the two hundred years since the Portuguese had first visited Africa in the 1680s. Local African businessmen formed alliances with Europeans and traded gold and ivory for textiles and alcohol. As Europeans learned African ways, some Africans, like Prince Aniaga of Guinea, became more European. Aniaga visited Paris and even became a respected captain in the French military before deciding to go home.

B. The Slave Trade on the African Coast

Led by the Dutch, most of the European powers had created outposts along an 8,000-mile stretch of the western coast of Africa. Embracing diverse geographic regions, this coastline was home to many distinct cultures of African tribes. Generations of Africans had become accustomed to contact with the Europeans, learning their languages and initiating trade.

Some traders from the interior of the continent, aware of the need for slaves in the New World, would make yearly treks to these coastal outposts with thousands of captive natives from tribal wars to sell to the Europeans. Sold slaves were then ferried across the Atlantic to the American colonies or the Caribbean.

C. The Middle Passage Experience

Lasting as much as two years, the deportation of a captured African to America was a harsh affair usually experienced in five distinct stages, beginning with initial capture in the interior of Africa and relocation to the coastal outposts.

The next stage included sale of the natives by African traders to Europeans. This transaction usually included close inspection of the slaves and identification branding into the skin. Confused and disoriented, slaves would lose track of relatives and friends by the time they reached the Atlantic. Great sailing vessels waited to be filled with slaves offshore.

Once filled, a transport's captain would make an educated guess about when to sail for America along the middle passage of the Atlantic. Factors such as weather, prior instructions from financiers, advice from local agents, and food supply contributed to a captain's decision to start the risky voyage.

The African slaves in these ships were kept in deplorable conditions, shackled side-by-side below decks. Filth and disease were the norm on the voyage and many slaves died on the way, only to be tossed overboard by the white crew or used as shark bait to help feed those who would survive.

D. Saltwater Slaves Arrive in America

The slaves unfortunate enough to survive the hellish sea journey were sold to individual planters, merchants, or speculators soon after arriving in America. The healthiest were paraded in their chains for inspection by the wealthy buyers. Those not sold immediately were advertised in the press.

Bought slaves were then transported to their permanent labor camps. Usually arriving in fall or winter, the new arrivals were indoctrinated into the life of a slave during a final stage known as "seasoning." This process was designed to allow the slave time to recover from the colossal shock of deportation and to heal physically.

IV. Survival in a Strange New Land

A. African Rice Growers in South Carolina

Unlike the Chesapeake region where slavery slowly replaced white labor, South Carolina depended on black slaves from its inception. South Carolina's climate and its hazards were similar to those in Africa. Working with cattle was also familiar to some slaves, while others were faced with unfamiliar tasks. Slaves were expected to produce their own food, and many turned to rice cultivation, common in their homelands.

Owners recognized the market opportunities of rice cultivation as food for slave populations in the Caribbean and later as a viable export to satisfy the European taste for rice pudding. Another labor intensive African product, indigo, also developed into a highly desirable dye for English textile industries.

B. Patterns of Resistance

South Carolina laws quickly emerged to protect owner interests, similar to the laws found in the Caribbean region. The strict working conditions and subsequent punishments did not develop a totally subservient people. Work slow-downs, faked illness, lost or broken tools, running away, and threats of violence were only some of the acts of resistance that slowly forced individual owners to alter working conditions. Slaves needed to calculate the reaction to such resistance, since punishments could be severe, and included confinement, reduction in food, whipping, mutilation, sale, or even death.

Owners feared their slaves and constantly watched for signs of a violent uprising of numbers of slaves or changes in activity of an angered individual who could strike out by burning fields at harvest time, destroying livestock, intentionally damaging expensive equipment, or murdering white owners or overseers.

C. A Wave of Rebellion

Individual acts of slave protest were common, yet group uprisings also occurred. During the 1730s, rumors of slave uprisings shook French Louisiana. Several suspected plotters were unsuccessfully tortured to force them to reveal the extent of the plot and names of others involved. They were then executed.

The largest colonial uprising, called the Stono Rebellion, occurred in South Carolina in 1739, shortly after the declaration of war between Spain and Britain. Approximately 70 armed slaves burned selected plantations, murdered ten whites, and tried to attract new recruits as they traveled toward the freedom promised in St. Augustine, Florida. Colonists and their Indian allies defeated the rebels before they reached Florida, while additional blacks suspected of rebel sympathies were tortured or killed during the wave of hysteria following the event. Charleston stopped another rumored uprising in 1740 by hanging the 50 suspects as an object lesson to other slaves.

New York also exploded in violent racial activity during fears generated by the Spanish war with England. Suspicious fires resulted in aggressive arrests and 34 executions and the expulsion of 72 free blacks from the town. It is clear that as slavery became imbedded in colonial life, white slave owners and neighboring colonists without slaves had serious concerns about their own safety.

V. The Transformation Completed

Those southern Americans who saw slavery as a viable tool for survival and success tightened the regulations concerning slave behavior, supported costly slave patrols and slave-catching activity, and sought to further control or drive from their midst the small but growing number of free blacks in their neighborhood. Free blacks in the North also faced increasing discrimination in relation to jobs and housing. The number of slaves also increased in the North, where slaves were most often used as servants, both to alleviate white mistresses from burdensome household tasks and to provide evidence of wealth and culture. Northern speculators and ship owners became wealthy by transporting slaves from Africa and selling them in the South.

A. Second-Class Status in the North

As Southern slave owners intimidated the enslaved Africans, African Americans in the North faced many similar problems. As slavery expanded, many whites saw free blacks as a threat and in 1691, Virginia restricted manumissions. As Southern slave colonies oppressed free blacks, in the North, discrimination against African Americans became widespread. Slavery continued and even strengthened in Northern colonies while white Christians lacked the will to fight against slavery. Even critics of the slave system, like Samuel Sewell of Massachusetts, were often ambivalent about the prospects for free blacks.

B. Is this Consistent "with Christianity or Common Justice"?

Although not all Americans condoned slavery, few even among religious leaders spoke out against the growing institution. Some religious leaders and philanthropists such as Thomas Bray promoted Christian instruction for slaves, which received little support among masters. Those who did give permission insisted that slaves be taught about their duties and clearly instructed that rewards or freedom would be found in heaven but not on earth. Among Quakers, individual opposition to slavery existed, but the church supported the individual's right to own slaves.

C. Oglethorpe's Antislavery Experiment

In 1731, the London proprietors of Georgia posed an idealistic challenge to southern slavery. The objective of this new colony was to provide a means of rescuing the worthy poor and those in jail for minor crimes by providing small farms as well as transportation to Georgia. In return, these new farmers would produce warm-weather items such as grapes and silk for the English market. This prosperous region would also provide a military buffer between Spanish Florida and South

Carolina. The proprietors took no profits from the colony but sought to control all aspects of its growth. Most important, Governor James Oglethorpe was dedicated to the cause of making Georgia a free-white colony with no slavery and no admission of free Africans.

Settlers in Georgia, whether from England, Germany, Switzerland, or Austria, faced the common adjustment problems to weather, geographic conditions, and animal and insect hazards encountered by all other new colonists. Resentment over the lack of a legislature enjoyed by the other English colonies and over the inability to buy or sell land or deed their land to whomever they desired to prevent the accumulation of large estates caused problems. In addition, the banning of slavery in the colony was viewed as a threat by other southern colonies.

D. The End of Equality in Georgia

Finally, a small, well-organized Georgia faction, joined by supporters from South Carolina, encouraged a rift among the proprietors about the appropriate course for the development of the colony. After holding out for two decades, slavery was allowed by 1751, and land-hungry South Carolinians pushed into Georgia to extend their slave empires into the rich, virgin soil. African slaves rapidly became the workers of choice, and Georgia laws controlling slavery mirrored the harsh statutes passed in South Carolina.

Identification

Explain the significance of each of the following:

1. The *Asiento:*

2. Bess Key:

3. Aniaga:

4. freedom dues:

5. Reverend Morgan Godwyn:

6. Bacon's Rebellion:

7. William Byrd:

8.   Negro Act of 1705:

9.   Barbados:

10.   Prince Rupert:

11.   Royal African Company:

12.   manumissions:

13.   triangular trade:

14.   "entrepots":

15.   coffle:

16.   barracoons:

17.   saltwater slaves:

18:   "seasoning":

19.   Sullivan's Island (Charleston):

20.   rice:

21.   indigo:

22.   Stono Rebellion:

23.   New York Slave Plot:

24.   Thomas Bray:

25.   Christian Priber:

26.   John Woolman:

27.   James Oglethorpe:

Multiple Choice Questions:

1.   Historians estimate that _____ people were enslaved and transported against their will to the Caribbean and Central, South, and North America.
    A.   50 million
    B.   100 million
    C.   25 million
    D.   15 million
    E.   10 million
    Page Reference: 114

2.   England became increasingly involved in the slave trade when the sugar colony of _____ began its economic take-off.
    A.   Barbados
    B.   Cuba
    C.   Trinidad
    D.   Puerto Rico
    E.   Haiti
    Page Reference: 106

3.   Black involvement in Bacon's Rebellion
    A.   was minimal and of little significance.
    B.   was almost exclusively made up of well-off free Blacks.
    C.   terrified the Dutch East Indies Company.
    D.   helped the slide of Virginia into race slavery.
    E.   took place on land owned by the East Indies Company Ltd.
    Page Reference: 111

4. Saltwater slaves were different than others in that they were
    A. used mostly as sailors.
    B. made to live in river shanties.
    C. working with crops that needed saltwater rather than fresh water.
    D. settled near the Atlantic Ocean.
    E. new to the country as opposed to slaves who were native born.
    Page Reference: 120

5. Roughly _____ Africans died at sea during the slave trade.
    A. 12,000,000
    B. 800,000
    C. 1,000,000
    D. 75,000
    E. 12,000
    Page Reference: 119

6. In their studies of the Middle Passage, historians have been able to document _____ slave voyages.
    A. 1,000
    B. 32,000
    C. 27,000
    D. 51,000
    E. 43,000
    Page Reference: 120

7. The final stage of Africans' journeys into slavery was called _____ and it gave them time to acclimate to their new worlds.
    A. the Long Dying
    B. seasoning
    C. the transition
    D. Middle Passage
    E. New Birth
    Page Reference: 120

8. The highest proportion of enslaved workers in North America lived in
    A. New York.
    B. Massachusetts.
    C. Georgia.
    D. Virginia.
    E. South Carolina.
    Page Reference: 122

9. West African slaves brought with them the profitable staple crop that transformed the South Carolina economy. It was
   A. rice.
   B. tobacco.
   C. indigo.
   D. sugar.
   E. corn.
   Page Reference: 123

10. Which of the following is NOT associated with African American music?
    A. jazz
    B. baroque music
    C. the banjo
    D. Blues
    E. Gospel
    Page Reference: 124

MAP QUESTION:

After looking at the information associated with Map 4.2, what general conclusions can you draw about the African slave trade and the European powers that perpetuated it?

CONNECTING HISTORY

Consider the question of slave reparations. In what way could this be accomplished fairly for everyone? Who would foot the bill? Should a generation of taxpayers who have never experienced slavery pay for the sins of a relatively few long-dead planters and merchants? Is granting reparations the only possible solution?

INTERPRETING HISTORY

Considering the time in which the plea to Bishop Gibson was written, what measures could the Church of England have followed to help the plight of the African slaves beyond Christianization? Were any measures feasible, considering the drastic need for labor in the colonies?

ENVISIONING HISTORY

What role did music play in providing African slaves a tool to survive their oppression? Explain how this worked and give examples.

THE WIDER WORLD

What does the odyssey of Job Ben Solomon tell about the ruthless nature of the slave trade?

Answers to Multiple Choice Questions

1. E
2. A
3. D
4. E
5. B
6. C
7. B
8. E
9. A
10. B

Chapter 5
An American Babel,
1713–1763

Learning Objectives:

After reading Chapter 5, you should be able to:

1. Understand the challenges many Indian nations faced from European animals and trade-goods long before they encountered Europeans themselves.
2. Explain why horses and guns were the most significant exchanges between Europeans and Indians.
3. Discuss which tribes of Native Americans were dominant in the different regions of the continent.
4. Discuss the root causes of the Indian wars.
5. Analyze how the Great Awakening altered the religious landscape of white America.
6. Explain how and why the French formed alliances with Indian tribes.

Time Line

1690
Arrival of the horse in the Comancheria

1700
Population of England at 5.1 million
Population of British North America at 260,000

1706
First Spanish contact with the Comanche
Benjamin Franklin born in Boston

1710
Inhaled snuff became popular among Europeans, creating more demand for colonial tobacco

1723
Benjamin Franklin, age 23, arrived in Philadelphia and began printing business

1737
Thomas Penn's Walking Purchase

1739

Revivalist George Whitefield visited America; his preaching ushered in the Great Awakening
Pierre and Paul Mallet set out to explore the Missouri River, tributary of the Mississippi

1740

Great Wagon Road used for wagon transportation from Philadelphia to South Carolina Piedmont

1742

Richmond, Virginia incorporated

1747

Ohio Company of Virginia founded

1749

Apache tribe established non-aggression pact with the Spanish

1750

Population of England at 5.8 million
Population of British North America at 1.2 million

1751

Georgia colony legalized slavery

1754

Skirmish between French and colonial forces under Major George Washington

1755

Eviction of French colonials from Acadia, British Nova Scotia; many moved to Louisiana to become Cajuns

1763

Treaty of Paris negotiated, ending hostilities in America and removing the French as a threat

1780

Comanche population grew to over 20,000

Chapter Overview

The term that best described the colonies of North America in the first half of the eighteenth century was "diverse." After the initial shock of contact, the native populations reorganized themselves in the West. New immigrant groups arrived from Europe, bringing with them new beliefs, ideas, and skills. The economic landscape became more varied and regionally specialized. As the colonists struggled with change, religious revivals swept across the cultural landscape while European power struggles cost France its Canadian empire.

I. New Cultures on the Western Plains

A. The Spread of the Horse

As the horse spread northward from Spanish settlements in New Mexico, French, and British trade guns slowly moved down from Canada or across the Mississippi River. Plains tribes like the Cheyenne and Crow in the Northern Plains and the Comanche in the Southern Plains, formerly dependent on dogs to aid village movement, readily adapted the horse, initially to carry burdens like the dog and then to improve bison-hunting expeditions.

Once the herds had increased, horses became key to raiding and warfare strategies. Social, religious, hunting, and raiding customs quickly adapted to the use of the horse. With hunting success came population increase, which in turn encouraged raids against distant enemies to acquire horses or other trade goods and to gain warrior status and leadership skills. The power of existing warrior societies increased and tribes without formal societies created them. Eventually, some of the sedentary tribes, like the Osage and Pawnee, chose to leave their riverside villages and agricultural lands for the nomadic life on the plains to remove their people from the constant slave raiding expeditions of their enemies.

B. The Rise of the Comanche

In the Southern Plains, the Comanche expanded their range from western Kansas to central Texas. Skilled warriors and hunters, their raids on Apache and Pueblo towns concerned the Spanish authorities. The presence of French traders at Natchitoches and New Orleans, territory claimed by Spain, also alarmed the Spanish authorities. The failure of Spanish expeditions to chastise the Comanche encouraged their raiding, which in turn meant Apache villages made more raids on Pueblo and Spanish settlements.

C. Creation of the Comacheria on the Southern Plains

To survive under the new pressures, Spanish villages made separate peace and trade agreements with the Comanche and Apache, increasing their own safety but also increasing the problems for other Spanish and Pueblo towns in the region. In two decades, the Comancheria encompassed most of Texas, with a tribal population of 20,000, and was to remain a powerful force in the Southwest for decades.

D. The Expansion of the Sioux

In the Northern Plains, the Beaver Wars and the impact of trade guns resulted in Sioux bands moving out onto the Plains. Familiarity with firearms gave the Sioux an advantage over western tribes, while access to horses significantly changed Sioux culture. The abundance of food increased band size, while the abundance of hides resulted in larger teepees and the accumulation of personal possessions.

The workload for women increased, as did their exposure to raiding parties. Leadership within the tribe shifted to include more hunters and warriors, while the influence of women and older men on tribal decisions decreased. Wealth was judged by the size of horse herds, and the need to pasture the expanding herds increased the necessity of constant movement.

II. Britain's Mainland Colonies: A New Abundance of People

A. Population Growth on the Home Front

Early marriage, the abundance of food, the need for laborers, and the relatively low occurrence of deadly epidemics due to population dispersal all contributed to an astonishing population growth in the American colonies. Families needed to be large to produce adequate labor for the parents. Benjamin Franklin, born in Boston in 1706, grew up in a household of 17 children that had all survived the frequent early death experienced by European children and colonial children a century before.

Most importantly, low death rate and a growing average life span contributed to the booming population of the American colonies. Food was plentiful, and the craftsmanship of housing improved dramatically. Newborns who survived infancy could expect to live a long life.

B. "Packed Like Herrings": Arrivals from Abroad

Immigration also added to colonial growth. From England came large numbers of independent persons pursuing opportunity or joining relatives. Many deported felons came as well, having been offered by the Crown the opportunity to work for a contracted length of time in America in return for dismissal of their prison sentences.

The British administration also sought to recruit Europeans, hoping that townships of acceptable ethnic groups on the colonial frontier would create a buffer against unwelcome Indian attacks. Immigrants were often offered sizable plots of land and free passage to America. However, despite these enticements, the African slave population continued to expand more quickly than the free community.

C. Non-English Newcomers in the British Colonies

Colonies that had begun existence as exclusively English became much more diverse after 1700. Much of the diversity was due to the Atlantic slave trade. By 1750, about 250,000 African Americans made up 20 percent of the English colonial population.

Native Americans accounted for a small number of the total, but the bulk of the colonial population was of European descent. Many spoke English with varying accents or not at all. The New England colonies remained the most homogenous, but even they experienced wide diversification of population during this period.

The majority of European immigrants were indentured servants. Sizeable numbers arrived from Scotland, Wales, and Germany. African slaves were more predominant in the South, arriving at a rate of some 4,000 per year, in some areas exceeding the white population.

III. The Varied Economic Landscape

Five distinct economic regions emerged in colonial America as local commercial systems gained strength and chose logical specialties. Transportation improved somewhat, but the colonies remained largely isolated. This led to regional diversification based upon immigration and agricultural and societal influence.

A. Sources of Gain in the Southeast

Two distinct regions emerged in the colonial Southeast. One centered on the low country of the South Carolina Piedmont, where warm weather produced a long growing season. Mild winters meant that livestock could forage independently all year long.

Some of the incoming slaves to the region had grown rice in Africa for years and continued the practice for their own consumption after arriving in America. Observing the African technique, regional planters realized the potential for revenue and devoted huge areas of cleared swamp for rice cultivation. Indigo also emerged as a staple crop for the region.

In North Carolina, a second region of agricultural economy evolved. Coastal geography compelled colonists to use the giant pine forests of the region for their profit. The pine trees yielded an abundance of the tar and pitch that were crucial to the shipbuilding industry. Slaves hauled the cut lumber and rendered pine sap to the coastal port of Wilmington, where dozens of sawmills processed the trees.

B. Chesapeake Bay's Tobacco Economy

North of the Carolina region, the entrenched colonies bordering Chesapeake Bay continued to cultivate tobacco as the primary staple crop despite a long decline in price at market. After 1710, inhaled snuff became widely popular in Europe, saving the regional economy. Consistent tobacco cultivation in the region began to deplete the soil and produce smaller yields, prompting the introduction of wheat and corn as secondary staple crops.

C. New England Takes to the Sea

North of the Bay area, two overlapping economies emerged. The New England colonies, long-established but less affluent than other regions, had not found a staple crop capable of flourishing in the rocky soil. All the reserves of beaver pelts had been harvested and most of the scarce fertile land was taken, and each successive generation had less land to pass along as the population swelled. With little hope for agriculture, a generation of New Englanders turned to the sea for a living.

Shipbuilding was successful in the region with shipyards lining the mouths of the major rivers. Whaling became a ready source of income as the blubber from the whales was found to be a stable fuel for lamps. Traditional fishing also flourished off the Grand Banks. As the region matured, men increased their influence in the political and business worlds, while women remained locked in gendered work and social patterns and retained their legal status as non-persons.

D. Economic Expansion in the Middle Colonies

The middle colonies—the fifth economic region—was situated between New England and the Chesapeake. The region enjoyed good weather and had an abundance of fertile land, which was put to use producing grain. The farmers exported wheat, flour, and bread to the rest of America and Europe. Unlike Virginia and its reliance on slaves, the middle colonies found a better balance and emphasized the use of paid labor. The seaports of New York and Philadelphia grew quickly with the influx of European trade.

Unfortunately, with the growth of the regional cities came the attendant poverty and other urban problems. Hospitals and asylums began to overflow. The answer seemed to be removing as many settlers as possible to the countryside or frontier, which continually pushed west. Thomas Penn, son and heir of Pennsylvania founder William Penn, made a point of defrauding the Delaware Indians in the Walking Purchase.

IV. Matters of Faith: The Great Awakening

A. Seeds of Religious Toleration

The same diversity that spread throughout the colonies brought with it a mix of religious cultures and creeds. There were representative numbers of Presbyterians, Quakers, Lutherans, Baptists, Methodists, Catholics, Jews, and many others.

The overall mindset of the colonies was one of inclusive toleration of religion. Only the Anglican Church caused suspicion, as most governors and wealthy colonists were members. A plan to install an Anglican bishop in the colonies was thwarted by other colonists fearful of an established religious hierarchy headed by the king of England.

B. The Onset of the Great Awakening: Pietism and George Whitefield

The relative religious toleration of the colonies provided a haven for many European religious sects. Collectively, these immigrants were part of a European reformation of Protestants in an age of rationalism and reason. Pietism—as this reformation was called—sought to renew vitality of worship and emphasize emotion and intensity in sects that had become stagnant.

George Whitefield became a leading proponent of Pietism in England. He visited the colonies several times, preaching a fervent message of inclusion for all believers and disdain for the structural obsessions of established religions. His message, delivered at just the right time, served as a catalyst of religious zeal in the colonies.

C. The Danger of an Unconverted Ministry

Local religious revivals had taken place in the colonies decades before the message of Pietism. Massachusetts theologian Jonathan Edwards argued that mechanical recitation of ritual was a poor substitute for a relationship with God.

In the colonies, the question of ongoing education for the subsequent generations of ministers arose as the few established colleges of theology were unable to produce enough qualified graduates to minister to the entire colonial population. The result was vacant pulpits throughout America. A contemporary of Whitefield, Gilbert Tennet, issued a printed sermon that blasted incompetent, uncaring, and greedy ministers and became a leading issue for the Awakening.

D. The Consequences of the Great Awakening

This Great Awakening of the American religious consciousness produced converts called "New Lights," who clashed with the conventional clergy supported by colonial governors. No unified church emerged from this energetic movement; instead, numerous congregations split off from existing churches and religious vigor blurred class lines and strained the conventional distance that had developed in America between politics and religion. The Great Awakening legacy of democratic associations and free thinking would prove valuable in the development of revolutionary ideology.

V. The French Lose a North American Empire

A. Prospects and Problems Facing French Colonists

By 1740, the size of French claims in North America above the Rio Grande exceeded those of Britain and Spain. Good relations with native tribes were a pivotal part of the fur trade empire. French trading forts dotted the interior, and explorers had also discovered the wealth of farmland that could be readily developed into thriving French towns and villages. Far fewer colonists immigrated to New France than to the British colonies, and the French government did not seriously back such immigration.

B. British Settlers Confront the Threat from France

England and France had long been in each other's way in North America. American colonists, beginning to feel the crowding of immigration, began to gauge the potential of the bountiful land west of the Appalachian mountains and speculate about what means might be necessary to oust the French. A group of colonial land brokers formed the Ohio Company of Virginia, seeking permission from the English king to develop these western lands. The king obliged and the members of the company made plans to erect a fort on the site of present-day Pittsburgh.

In a skirmish in 1754, a group of colonial militia (headed by Major George Washington) killed ten French soldiers who would not leave the proposed fort site, aiming to claim the land for their own country. This skirmish launched fears of a French attack throughout the colonies. Benjamin Franklin proposed a joint coalition of colonial militia tasked with building defensive forts and actively repelling any French invasion. Further skirmishes pushed at the coalition soldiers, leaving the colonial governors no choice but to beg the Crown for help in repelling the French and their Native American allies.

The Crown dispatched General Edward Braddock and two regiments of infantry, which arrived in the colonies in 1755. The combined British and colonial armies marched west to meet the French.

C. An American Fight Becomes a Global Conflict

Unfortunately, the aging General Braddock proved to be incompetent. The French and Indian forces attacked his column at will, delivering a costly defeat. In England, the new ministry of William Penn helped to change British and colonial fortunes. His plan was to concentrate remaining British force on the under-populated, world-wide colonial holdings of the French.

The superior British Navy began bombardments in Asia, Africa, and North America. Diverted, the French turned their attention overseas while fresh supplies and troops arrived from England. The next spring found the British forces pressing the French into Canada, eventually conquering Fort Niagara, the easternmost French stronghold. This effectively choked the rest of the French arsenal in North America.

D. Quebec Taken and North America Refashioned

By 1760, France had lost Quebec and Montreal, signaling final French defeat in America. The war continued overseas, finally ending in the Treaty of Paris in 1763. Under the provisions of the treaty, the French ceded New Orleans and the Louisiana territory west of the Mississippi to Spain. Spain ceded East Florida to Britain. France ceded all claims between the Appalachian Mountains and the Mississippi River and all remaining claims in Canada in exchange for British return of the French sugar islands in the Caribbean. Unexpectedly, France made no provisions to protect the lands of its Indian allies. French presence in America effectively disappeared overnight.

Identification

Explain the significance of each of the following:

1.   horses:

2.   guns:

3.   travois:

4.   counting coup:

5. The Comancheria:

6. *mazawakan:*

7. Benjamin Franklin:

8. redemption contract:

9. Acadians:

10. The Great Wagon Road:

11. rice:

12. Moravians:

13. slave societies:

14. Overseers of the Poor:

15. Walking Purchase:

16. Bettering House:

17. The Great Awakening:

18. George Whitefield:

19. John Wesley:

20.	Gilbert Tennet:

21.	New Lights:

22.	Old Lights:

23.	Pierre Mallet:

24.	The Ohio Company of Virginia:

25.	William Pitt:

Multiple Choice Questions:

1.	The French Protestants who fled to English North America at the end of the seventeenth century were called
	A.	Jews.
	B.	Mennonites.
	C.	Quakers.
	D.	Lutherans
	E.	Huguenots.
	Page Reference: 145

2.	The rise of the Comanche was based more than anything else on the
	A.	development of settled agriculture.
	B.	use of the railroads.
	C.	friendly relations with the French.
	D.	discovery of gold on their land.
	E.	horse.
	Page Reference: 139

3.	Early colonial commerce was greatly facilitated by extensive
	A.	river networks.
	B.	roads.
	C.	railroads.
	D.	bridges.
	E.	canals.
	Page Reference: 148

4. Many Scots-Irish and German families left the middle colonies for the Carolinas and Georgia via the
    A. Atlantic seaboard.
    B. Mississippi River.
    C. Great Wagon Road.
    D. Baltimore and Chesapeake Railroad.
    E. Cape Fear River.
    Page Reference: 150

5. After a long decline in market price, tobacco prices rebounded in the early eighteenth century because of its use as
    A. a stimulant.
    B. fertilizer.
    C. a painkiller.
    D. snuff.
    E. All of the above.
    Page Reference: 151

6. Off Cape Cod, Whaling became a new source of income because
    A. whale products were needed for cotton production.
    B. whale blubber could be turned into oil.
    C. of the slave trade.
    D. indentured servitude supplied lots of cheap labor.
    E. farming could not feed the population of New England.
    Page Reference: 152

7. The middle colonies' most reliable staple crop was
    A. grain.
    B. tobacco.
    C. grapes.
    D. indigo.
    E. oranges.
    Page Reference: 154

8. The religious revivalism that swept colonial America in the early eighteenth century was called the
    A. Great Revival.
    B. Family Values campaign.
    C. Great Awakening.
    D. Great Tolerance.
    E. Outpouring.
    Page Reference: 155

9. The French Colonies in North America suffered from
    A. following the Roman Catholic faith.
    B. being too nice to the Indians.
    C. not exploring the interior of North America enough.
    D. lack of population.
    E. the Lutheran church.
    Page Reference: 160

10. The Seven Years War that ended in 1763 cost _____ its colonial empire in North America.
    A. Holland
    B. France
    C. Spain
    D. England
    E. Portugal
    Page Reference: 165

MAP QUESTION:

Study Map 5.2 regarding the economic regions of the British colonies. Are there any specifics about the regions that still hold true today?

CONNECTING HISTORY

Why might a concerned government such as the federal government of the United States place few restrictions on the amount of noise we have to endure every day? What could be done to return our country to a state of high fidelity?

INTERPRETING HISTORY

Is the passage "Pastures Can Be Found Almost Everywhere" written objectively, or does it contain persuasive elements?

ENVISIONING HISTORY

What does the story of Mary Jemison say about race and gender in eighteenth century colonial America?

THE WIDER WORLD

Explain the problem of longitude at sea and how it impacted the colonization of North America.

Answers to Multiple Choice Questions

1. E
2. E
3. A
4. C
5. D
6. B
7. A
8. C
9. D
10. B

Chapter 6
The Limits of Imperial Control,
1763–1775

Learning Objectives:

After reading Chapter 6, you should be able to:

1. Explain the different challenges to expansion that Spain faced at the hands of the other European powers.
2. Discuss the expansion of the British Empire and what challenges were encountered.
3. Detail the problems England faced after the Seven Years' War and what steps Parliament took to correct the economy.
4. Relate a timetable of events demonstrating the breakdown of relations between the colonies and the English Crown.
5. Discuss the colonial boycott of English imported goods and how the Crown reacted.
6. Explain colonial mob violence and the progression of events leading to warfare.

Time Line:

1741
Vitus Bering claimed Alaska for Russia

1760
French forces surrendered to British at Montreal in final skirmish of the Seven Years' War

1763
Spain acquired Louisiana from France
Britain acquired Florida from Spain
Pontiac's Uprising, Detroit

1764
Parliament passed the American Duties Act of 1764, also known as the Revenue Act or the Sugar Act
Parliament passed the Currency Act of 1764

1765
Parliament passed the Quartering Act
Stamp Act passed, resulting in the dissenting Stamp Act Congress in New York

1766
Louis Bougainville made first French circumnavigation of the world
Parliament repealed the Stamp Act, passed Declaratory Act, Revenue Act of 1766

1767
Parliament passed Revenue Act of 1767, Customs Act of 1767

1768
Massachusetts legislature, led by Samuel Adams, petitioned the king for redress of colonial complaints
Massacre of St. George's Field, London

1769
Spain established an outpost at San Diego Bay on the California coast

1770
Townsend Duties repealed save for the one on tea
Boston Massacre

1772
Gaspee Affair

1773
Committees of Correspondence formed in 11 colonies
Tea Act of 1773
Boston Tea Party

1774
Four Coercive Acts passed by Parliament to punish Massachusetts:
    -Administration of Justice Act
    -Boston Port Act
    -The Quartering Act
    -Massachusetts Government Act
Also passed Quebec Act; all five together constituted the Intolerable Acts
Minutemen formed
First Continental Congress

1775
Spain populated San Francisco Bay area
Second Continental Congress
Battles of Lexington and Concord
"Shot heard 'round the world"

1778
British explorer James Cook discovered Hawaiian Islands

1781
Yuma Revolt near Colorado River

1812

Alexander Baranov established a Russian outpost on the California coast near San Francisco

Chapter Overview

As the European empires of Spain and Britain struggled with acute growing pains, American colonists bridled at imperial controls. The English Crown attempted to force the colonies to pay for themselves while colonists lashed out at the arbitrariness of central authority. By the 1770s, events began to spin out of control, carrying the American colonies towards revolution.

I. New Challenges to Spain's Expanded Empire

With the vexing problem of refuting French claims to Louisiana settled, the Spanish regained nominal control of the American interior from the Mississippi to the Pacific Ocean. Tribes still controlled the land in reality, however, and it became clear that other nations remained interested in the region. Increasing problems with Russian, French, and British naval and trade expeditions along the Pacific coast prompted Spain to expand her mission/presidio system northward along the California coast.

A. Pacific Exploration, Hawaiian Contact

Burdened with a crushing war debt after the loss of the Seven Years' War, the French looked to the South Pacific for other sources of revenue. In 1766, Antoine de Bougainville set out to search for new territory; while unsuccessful, he became the first Frenchman to circumnavigate the globe.

Always competitive, the British sent out their own series of explorers into the South Pacific. The most successful of these was James Cook, who came upon the populated Hawaiian Islands in 1778. The natives mistook the captain for a deity and welcomed him and his crew for an extended stay. A return visit in 1779 was not as successful; an angry crowd of Hawaiians killed Cook and four of his crew.

B. The Russians Lay Claim to Alaska

Using successful tactics developed in Siberia, Russian trappers used a combination of conquest and ransom to coerce Aleutian Islanders and Alaskan native peoples to hunt. In 1799, the czar gave the Russian-American Company exclusive rights to this trade. With strong outposts in Alaska, which had been claimed for Russia by Vitus Bering, the Russian-American Company worked south toward California, exploiting local trade opportunities and seeking appropriate climate and farmland to grow staples for the Alaskan trading posts. By 1812, Fort Ross, just north of San Francisco, became the southernmost Russian fort.

C. Spain Colonizes the California Coast

Franciscan priests established scattered Indian missions between San Diego and San Francisco. These settlements remained small, isolated, and difficult to supply. Provisioning by sea was not very successful, so Spanish expeditions sought for many years a dependable overland route. By doing so, Spain was accumulating solid legal grounds for claiming the land. This might have been enough to prevent encroachment by the powerful British, but it was not tested by war. The tiny California settlements endured, and Spain continued to exercise some control over its expanded American empire.

II. New Challenges to Britain's Expanded Empire

The peace at the end of the Seven Years' War, which brought wealth to a few and misery to many, produced growing tensions between colonial conservatives who enjoyed the rewards of the English class system and the majority of colonists who struggled to make ends meet. Some of the wealthy, ambitious young men sought another way to power by decreasing their distance from the lower class. During the next decade, the uncertain coalition between working men and these wealthy young men strengthened as their sense of a separate American identity developed into a new vision of America free from British rule.

A. Midwestern Lands and Pontiac's War for Indian Independence

On the frontier, the Delaware holy man, Neolin, and the influential Ottawa warrior, Pontiac, forged a coalition of Ottawas, Potawatomies, and Hurons, and attacked Fort Detroit and Fort Pitt. Eighteen other Indian nations joined the coalition to drive the British out of the native homelands. Britain lost all remaining forts in the Ohio Valley and Great Lakes region, and tribes raided eastward into Pennsylvania and Virginia. Settlers responded with indiscriminate racial killing.

British General Amherst ordered a war of extermination, using all means available, including the intentional spreading of smallpox using contaminated blankets. Unable to win the siege when their ammunition ran out, the Indian coalition slowly collapsed. English losses were so significant that the Crown forbade settlement west of the Appalachian Range to avoid further warfare. This so-called Proclamation Line of 1763 served mostly to anger upper class Virginians who made their living as land speculators. Additional treaties in following years only heightened the animosity of whites towards Indians.

B. Grenville's Effort at Reform

During the 1760s, England tried to develop better control over the American colonies, where tax evasion had become a way of life. England's war debt after the Seven Years' conflict was staggering and as the post-war economic depression deepened, England looked to its colonies for increased revenue. Parliament, under the leadership of Robert Grenville, passed new customs regulations and tax laws to help pay the expenses incurred in defending the colonies and to turn a modest profit.

The ministers were not anticipating a powerful reaction from the colonies to these measures, which began with the American Duties Act (increased duties on colonial products), followed closely with the Currency Act of 1764 (prohibited colonies from printing money), as well as a Quartering Act (compelled colonists to assist the British Army).

C. The Stamp Act Imposed

Grenville's most weighty reform, the Stamp Act (1765) was a complex measure of statutes requiring taxation stamps on a wide variety of articles sold in the colonies. This could include legal contracts and commissions, land deeds, liquor licenses, slave contracts, academic degrees, playing cards, and dice.

Designated colonial agents assigned by the Crown were intended to sell these stamps at a profit for themselves; however, the bulk of the revenue was intended for a separate account earmarked for the financial administration of America. Parliament was very pleased with this measure, which most ministers viewed as moderate and exceedingly fair. Better yet, revenue would grow with the colonial population since everyone used the taxed items from time to time.

D. The Stamp Act Resisted

American demonstrations against the Stamp Act were immediate and violent. Patrick Henry's speeches set a philosophical precedent for self-taxation. Massachusetts called for a Stamp Act Congress of the colonies to be held in New York to beg relief from Parliament. Angry mobs determined the names of stamp distributors and harassed them often forcing their resignation before the hated stamps even arrived from England. A few of these mobs began to organize and inflame the tempers of others. The most violent riot occurred in Boston, where Lieutenant Governor Thomas Hutchinson's house was looted and vandalized. South Carolina workers harassed wealthy slave owners with demands for liberty. However, when blacks took up the cry of liberty, white support for the demonstrations evaporated, lest white protests should fuel slave revolts.

III. "The Unconquerable Rage of the People"

A. Power Corrupts: An English Framework for Revolution

When discussions in England over the nature of monarchy turned to abuse of or the rise of tyranny, the assumption was that the empowerment of Parliament during the Glorious Revolution had ended these fears, yet constant vigilance was needed to protect citizens' rights.

Englishmen congratulated themselves on having achieved the perfect balance of government. However, a few dissenting voices in England published broadsides on the injustice of the patronage system for civil servants, a system rife with corruption. Although these writers were largely ignored in Britain, their message fell on eager ears in the colonies, where such discussions generated alarm and heated debate among those who saw class tyranny and malfeasance of office already evident in America.

B. Americans Practice Vigilance and Restraint

Fearing that every individual act of corruption represented a dangerous precedent, American colonists felt they must be alert, if circumspect. First, all legal means of appeal and redress must be utilized. Even if forced to the streets, crowds should be orderly and threaten property before people. In the main, protests against the Stamp Act showed this restraint.

C. Rural Unrest: Tenant Farmers and Regulators

After 1765, local unrest seemed to explode in the more rural areas where most of the colonists lived. Numerous examples of uprisings are archived, all of which had to be suppressed by British troops. Tenant farmers seemed to carry the most anger, since taxation and the Stamp Act had hit them the hardest, and those with little have not much to lose.

Violence shook the Carolina Piedmont, where lawlessness ruled scant miles from the inhabited coast. In inland North Carolina, a corrupt elite developed with the fledgling circuit court system, an elite connected with political and financial muscle farther east and north. Appointed to various posts by the colonial governor, this elite seemed intolerable and self-serving to newcomers from Virginia and Pennsylvania.

These newcomers, in search of fertile land, grew in number and banded together to speak out for better representation for the backcountry areas in the colonial assemblies. They began organizing into groups called Regulators. Their worst suspicions about the corruption of government were confirmed with the news that public funds would go to build a stately mansion for the colonial governor. Colonists like the Regulators would bear the cost of this mansion but few would ever see its location far east on the coast. Hundreds of backcountry families joined the growing Regulator movement in protest of this betrayal of the public wealth. In 1771, the governor finally called out a thousand men of the colonial militia and sent them into the Piedmont. Leaders of the Regulators were hanged and the majority of members were forced to sign loyalty oaths.

IV. A Conspiracy of Corrupt Ministers?

Class and religion continued to divide the colonists, sometimes leading to armed conflict. The biggest diversion to the infighting was the colossal corruption of the English government. Reflective colonists had to wonder if there existed a conspiracy against them and the few liberties they retained.

A series of weak ministries in London followed the administration of Grenville; however, Parliament was still keen on the colonial taxation issue. After repeal of the Stamp Act, the first outrage issued was the Revenue Act of 1766, which restructured the duty schedule for molasses. Grumbling, the colonists paid the duty, skeptically aware that doing so continued to set dangerous precedents.

They were correct, for Parliament was encouraged to impose additional hard-line measures, crafted by England's Chancellor of the Exchequer, Charles Townsend, in 1767. Taxation without representation was now a colonial reality.

A. The Townsend Duties

As always, the royal government was low on funds, prompting Townsend to initiate the first of the duties that bear his name. The Revenue Act of 1767 created new duties on imports to the colonies such as glass, paint, lead, paper, and tea. Proceeds were again earmarked for the administration of justice and support of the colonial civil government.

Colonial skeptics knew that administration of justice really meant license to search American shops and homes with hateful "writs of assistance" to uncover smuggled goods. "Support of civil government" actually meant that corrupt colonial administrators could draw arbitrary paychecks directly from the duties paid by colonists instead of relying on a system of local oversight.

Similar acts and outrages followed. Parliament directed colonial governors, now being paid directly from tax and duty funds, to ignore any colonial legislative measure regarding control of how members were chosen. The Customs Act of 1767 established a separate Board of Customs for all of British North America; with its new headquarters disquietingly near in Boston instead of London, the British would now have their fingers firmly on the pulse of American commerce. Several other Parliament actions strengthened the royal government's presence in the colonies and assured that the flow of revenue back to England would continue.

While most English subjects looked upon these Acts as efficient signs of good government, the colonists were outraged at the growing mountain of regulations set upon them. In 1768, the Massachusetts legislature, led by Samuel Adams, formally petitioned the king for redress of their complaints, prompted other colonial legislatures to do the same, and in a provocative "Circular Letter," condemned the hated Townsend Duties as taxation without representation.

B. Virtuous Resistance: Boycotting British Goods

Although emotions were high, colonial leaders managed to control most outbreaks of mob violence. Instead, they initiated a series of British boycotts, appealing to colonial self-sufficiency and non-violent protest. As the movement grew, women of all social classes made, sold and dressed in homemade clothing.

Local groups pledged to resist the temptation to buy imported tea or London fashions. In New York alone, imports from Britain dropped from 491,000 pounds sterling in value to a mere 76,000 in one year.

The effects of the boycotts proved damaging to the British, who began losing more in trade than was being made in duties. Wealthy English traders began pressuring Parliament for some relief, and in 1770, they were forced to repeal all the Townsend duties save the one on tea. This action defused the colonial boycotts but continued to confirm Parliament's right to tax the colonies at will.

C. The Boston Massacre

Tensions continued to mount in the colonies during 1768, especially in Boston where a reinforced garrison of British regulars kept order. According to revolutionary beliefs, any appearance of a standing army in peacetime meant danger, and the issue of how to feed and house 4,000 unwanted soldiers became an inflammatory one.

In 1770, the tension reached a zenith. When a hostile crowd threatened a British informer, he fired back, killing an eleven-year-old boy. A subsequent funeral brought multitudes of colonists into the streets for demonstrations. This became the pattern for days to come, and it was clear to all that confrontation was unavoidable. A tense standoff on March 5, outside the Boston customs house, resulted in the deaths of five colonists at the hands of the British soldiers. The anti-British cause had gained its first martyrs.

D. The *Gaspee* Affair Prompts Committees of Correspondence

As the 1770s wore on, Bostonians made a point of commemorating "Massacre Day" each year. The continued presence of the British troops and corrupt and overzealous customs officials helped fuel resentment of the British.

In June, 1772 the *Gaspee*, a customs boat rumored to harass local shipping, ran aground near Pawtucket, Rhode Island. That night, more than a hundred raiders rowed out to the stranded vessel, drove off its crew, and set the boat afire.

This incident renewed bitter relations between England and the colonies. The Crown demanded an investigation of the incident and extradition of the accused to England. The investigation went nowhere; many of the raiders came from influential Rhode Island families and local citizens were loathe to become informants in a process that denied the accused fundamental judicial rights. Committees of Correspondence were created in most colonial legislatures to serve as watchdogs against further infringement of rights.

V. Launching a Revolution

In 1767, before the inception of the Townsend duties, the colonies had imported 870,000 pounds of tea. Subsequent boycotts cut this amount to 110,000 pounds as colonists turned to smuggling or making root-based teas. Retraction of the boycotts in 1770 led to the resumption of the colonial purchase of English tea, although a duty remained in effect. Encouraged by these developments, the British government made plans to bail out the failing East India Company by liquidating the 18 million pounds of unsold tea in London warehouses.

A. The Tempest over Tea

In May, Parliament passed The Tea Act of 1773, which let the struggling East India Company bypass the costly requirement that all colonial imports had to come through England first. Any warehoused tea earmarked for the colonies would have its English duties refunded.

The company recruited a few local colonists to handle and distribute a planned 600,000 pounds of tea, for which they would be awarded 6 percent. The Sons of Liberty and other revolutionary groups vowed to keep the British tea ships from docking at colonial harbors, protesting the British insistence on taxation without representation.

In Boston, where tensions ran especially high in light of the Boston Massacre of five years past, the royal governor was determined to dock three approaching British ships heavy with British tea. As private firearms were scarce, the governor anticipated little need for force in unloading and distributing the tea cargo.

On December 16, following a prearranged plan, 150 men disguised as Indians with war hatchets marched to the docks and boarded the ships. As most of the citizenry looked on, these "Indians" spent most of the evening systematically breaking open the many chests of tea and dumping them overboard into the harbor. This act became a unifying event in the colonies and spurred similar acts of defiance against the British.

B. The Intolerable Acts

Parliament responded to the Boston Tea Party with measures meant to punish the city and assert English authority. General Gage, the commander of colonial British forces, replaced Governor Hutchinson as governor, effectively placing Massachusetts under martial law. In 1774, Parliament published the Coercive Acts—four statutes directed squarely at Massachusetts. The Boston Port Act enclosed Boston in a naval blockade until the cost of the ruined tea was paid off. The Administration of Justice Act allowed extradition of British citizens (such as those soldiers involved in the Boston Massacre) to other colonies or to England.

The Quartering Act gave British officers extended powers to commandeer living quarters and supplies for troops throughout the colonies. Finally, the Massachusetts Government Act removed certain democratic rhetoric from the Massachusetts Charter of 1691. Colonists would now have to obtain written permission from the colonial governor to have town meetings. Parliament went further, issuing the Quebec Act the same year; this measure vastly increased the official size of the Canadian holdings of England, effectively nullifying the claims of the colonies to western lands. Taken together, the Quebec Act and the Coercive Acts were known in the colonies as the Intolerable Acts, and ushered in a new phase of open rebellion against the Crown. Pamphlets were issued throughout the continent condemning the British and publicizing the plight of the Massachusetts colonists.

Within a few months, Massachusetts called for a congress of all the colonies, establishing its own revolutionary base in Concord, 17 miles from Boston. This base, known as the Massachusetts Provincial Congress, reorganized the local militia into loyal units ready to respond quickly to General Gage's repeated attempt to confiscate colonial gunpowder. This militia became known as the Minutemen.

C. From Words to Action

Extralegal organizations, representing a broad spectrum of political stances, began to vie for power in hundreds of colonial villages. Boycotts of English products continued in earnest and widespread support developed for Massachusetts' call for a unified congress. In 1774, all colonies except Georgia participated in the First Continental Congress in Philadelphia. This Congress managed to produce a Declaration of Rights and passed a range of measures that seemed a compromise of the wide convictions of the 56 delegates.

Most important, the delegates signed an agreement to resist British imports and halt all exports to London save for rice. They adjourned, calling for a Second Congress in 1775. Just before the date of the Second Congress, General Gage received orders from his English superiors to arrest the leaders of the Massachusetts Provincial Congress using any means at his disposal.

On April 18, 1775, Gage ordered a full regiment of English troops to row across the Charles River at night, march ten miles overland to Lexington, and there seize John Hancock and Sam Adams. Next, the soldiers were to march the seven miles to Concord to capture the colonial military supply depot.

Alerted by lanterns from the Old North Church, riders Paul Revere and William Dawes hurried along separate routes to Lexington to warn Hancock and Adams. By the time the English regulars arrived in Lexington, seventy Minutemen stood against them on the town green. Firing, the British felled eight militiamen in the skirmish.

The British column then turned west to Concord and searched for the military supplies concealed there. Four hundred Minutemen advanced from the overlooking hillside. At the small bridge over the Concord River, the British opened fire with "the shot heard 'round the world." The colonists returned fire and by noon caused the exhausted British to retreat with 73 killed and 100 wounded. The Americans—losing 49 men—had handed the British their first colonial defeat.

Identification

Explain the significance of each of the following:

1.   Louis Antoine de Bougainville:

2.   James Cook:

3.   Vitus Bering:

4.   *promyshlenniki*:

5.   The Russian-American Company:

6.   Alexander Baranov:

7.   Jose de Galvez:

8.   Father Garces:

9.   The Yuma Revolt:

10. Neolin:

11. Pontiac:

12. General Thomas Gage:

13. The Proclamation Line of 1763:

14. Robert Grenville:

15. American Duties Act of 1764:

16. The Currency Act of 1764:

17. The Quebec Act:

18. Exchequer:

19. Patrick Henry:

20. The Stamp Act Congress:

21. The Sons of Liberty:

22. Thomas Hutchinson:

23. Declaratory Act of 1766:

24. The Massacre of St. George's Field

25. Levellers:

26. Regulators:

27. Tyron's Palace:

28. Revenue Act of 1766:

29. The Townsend Duties:

30. The Boston Massacre:

31. The Boston Tea Party:

32. The Intolerable Acts:

33. Minutemen:

34. Concord, Massachusetts:

35. Paul Revere:

Multiple Choice Questions:

1. By the 1760s, Boston had become
    A. the city with the largest percentage of slaves living in it.
    B. a bedrock source of support for the British government.
    C. a busy seaport of 16,000 people.
    D. a place with very, very few wealthy citizens.
    E. All of the above.
    Page Reference: 167

2. Alaska was claimed by_____ for _____ in 1741.
    A. George Wythe; Britain
    B. Thomas Jefferson; Virginia
    C. Comte de Escargole; France
    D. George Washington; United States
    E. Vitus Bering; Russia
    Page Reference: 171

3. In response to Pontiac's War, General Amherst ordered
    A. his men to spread smallpox among the Indians and take no prisoners.
    B. a ban on the slave trade.
    C. an end to the whisky tax.
    D. religious restrictions on pagan Indians.
    E. a call for peaceful negotiation.
    Page Reference: 177

4. Colonial leaders borrowed many of their ideas about power and government from the
    A. "Real Whigs."
    B. Native Americans.
    C. Ancient Greeks.
    D. Russians.
    E. None of the above.
    Page Reference: 183

5. Trenchard and Gordon's *Cato's Letters*
    A. explained the official position of the British government.
    B. influenced American radicals with its critique of power.
    C. inspired the Stamp Act.
    D. offered a new plan of democratic government.
    E. was a defense of the slave trade.
    Page Reference: 184

6. Small farmers protested against regressive taxes that
   A. hurt wealthy real estate speculators.
   B. helped the political intriguers in the New York Assembly.
   C. punished merchants angry about the Stamp Act.
   D. imposed the same burden on all regardless of wealth.
   E. favored French traders.
   Page Reference: 185

7. The author of "Letters from a Farmer in Pennsylvania" was
   A. Patrick Henry.
   B. Charles Townshend.
   C. John Dickinson.
   D. Benjamin Franklin.
   E. William Penn, Jr.
   Page Reference: 187

8. The Townsend Duties were
   A. a guarantee of trial by jury.
   B. wildly greeted by colonial legislatures.
   C. the treaty that ended the Seven Years' War.
   D. a list of responsibilities for English citizens.
   E. taxes on lead, glass, paint, and tea.
   Page Reference: 188

9. One result of the movement to boycott British goods was
   A. a failure to have adequate clothing in the colonies.
   B. trade with Britain actually increased as Tories demonstrated their loyalty.
   C. colonial women made, sold, and wore garments they made themselves.
   D. massive profits for French merchants.
   E. violence broke out almost daily in major colonial port cities.
   Page Reference: 189

10. The so-called Intolerable Acts included
    A. the Tea Act.
    B. a Religious Toleration Act.
    C. a Non-Importation Act.
    D. the Boston Port Act.
    E. All of the above.
    Page Reference: 192

MAP QUESTION:

Look at Map 6.3, specifically the numerous keys marked "British forts seized during Pontiac's Rebellion in 1763." Under the prophet Neolin, interior tribes united to remove the British colonists from tribal lands. Why was the attempt unsuccessful?

CONNECTING HISTORY

Protest tactics are numerous and show up often in the study of history. What protest tactics have been covered in the news recently? Are they much different from those of the past? Which seem to be most effective? What type of protest would you consider too radical for your own participation?

INTERPRETING HISTORY

Explain why Tyron Palace generated such outrage from this group of "Regulators."

ENVISIONING HISTORY

Discuss how the various elements in Hogarth's painting makes comment on recent events in the colonies. How would various colonial groups react to this satire?

THE WIDER WORLD

Discuss how Captain Cook can be seen as a representative of rationalism and the enlightenment.

Answers to Multiple Choice Questions

1.   C
2.   E
3.   A
4.   A
5.   B
6.   D
7.   C
8.   E
9.   C
10. D

Chapter 7
Revolutionaries at War,
1775–1783

Learning Objectives:

After reading Chapter 7, you should be able to:

1. Discuss why it took the Continental Congress 15 months after the bloodshed at Lexington to declare war against England.
2. Explain the problems encountered by Washington in forming a new army.
3. Understand the role of the Continental Congress during the Revolutionary War.
4. Evaluate the problems that faced the civilian population during the Revolutionary War.
5. Appreciate the value of America's foreign allies during the Revolutionary War.
6. Understand the major events of the Revolutionary War and their consequences.
7. Explain why the Battle of Yorktown signaled the end of the Revolutionary War.

Time Line

1775
Second Continental Congress
George Washington appointed to command all continental forces, arrived in Cambridge to take command and oversee siege of Boston
Battle of Bunker Hill (Breed's Hill)
Gen. Montgomery's American troops seized Montreal
England's annual war expenditures: four million pounds, sterling
Birth of the American Navy

1776
Common Sense produced in Philadelphia by Thomas Paine
Washington secured Dorchester Heights, used captured British artillery to bombard Boston
Congress voted to approve the Declaration of Independence on July 4, 1776
Battle of Long Island
Washington crossed the Delaware River to Trenton
Battle of Princeton
Holland first country to recognize American sovereignty
Virginia adopted first state constitution

1777
Battle of Brandywine Creek
Both Battles of Freeman's Farm
Articles of Confederation approved (ratified by the states in 1781)
Washington at winter quarters in Valley Forge

1778
Friedrich von Steuben arrived at Valley Forge to train American troops
Congress approved alliance between America and France
English peace commission offered concessions to the Continental Congress
Battle of Monmouth

1779
Fort Wilson Riot
American alliance with Spain

1780
American alliance with Holland
Battle of King's Mountain
Nathaniel Greene replaced Gates as head of southern command

1781
Battle of Cowpens
Battle of Guilford Courthouse
British naval force repulsed by French fleet
British surrender at Yorktown

1782
British negotiated preliminary terms for peace with America

1783
Final peace treaty at Versailles, France

Chapter Overview

American revolutionaries declared their independence from England in 1776 only after arduous debate. By that time, the rebellion was struggling for survival. This chapter discusses the early battles, efforts to win European recognition for the new nation, and the final military defeat of the British armies at Yorktown.

I. "Things are Now Come to That Crisis"

A. The Second Continental Congress Takes Control

In the two months after the 1775 skirmishes at Lexington and Concord, the second Continental Congress sent aid north to Boston, placed Philip Schuyler in charge of the newly formed Army Department, printed its own currency, and appointed George Washington as commander of the Continental forces. During the same time, rebel forces captured Fort Ticonderoga in the Hudson Valley, while others put siege to Boston. Congress also approved a plan to attack Canada, to be led by General Robert Montgomery.

B. Liberty to Slaves

The choice of plantation-owner Washington as commanding general put limits on the possibilities for any coalition of the races in America. The move sent a strong message to the half-million African Americans that the Patriot cause might not have a place for them; this prompted some to risk siding with the British.

Southern slave owners feared the possible response of African Americans to a war between rebels and Britain. Although Virginia governor Lord Dunmore offered freedom to slaves of rebel masters who would fight for England, the rebel government made no similar offer, and most slaves remained unsure how this struggle would affect them.

C. The Struggle to Control Boston

In June, the British army successfully engaged rebel forces outside of Boston in the Battle of Breed's Hill (known popularly as Bunker Hill). Rebel forces under Montgomery and Arnold invaded Canada, taking Montreal but failing at Quebec. Other rebel forces under Washington continued to organize and train at Cambridge, waiting for the arrival of Henry Knox and the heavy siege guns captured from Ticonderoga in March. Unwilling to risk the destruction of Boston, the British fleet removed the army to Nova Scotia.

II. Declaring Independence

A. "Time to Part"

Thomas Paine's pamphlet *Common Sense*, a widely popular piece of mass persuasion, was published in January 1776. The simple, plain-spoken arguments for independence that Paine wrote generated such support that one colony after another instructed its representatives to vote for independence. Surprisingly, despite these activities, the Continental Congress debated taking the final step of formally declaring war on Britain.

After much debate, most members of the Congress concluded that accommodation from England would not be forthcoming and assigned a Committee of Five to prepare the formal document severing their political alliance with the Crown. The Declaration of Independence was created and approved 15 months after the shots were fired at Lexington.

B. The British Attack New York

While Congress debated, the British formulated plans to crush the rebellion. One such plan involved a southern strategy, resting on the assumption that the strongest support for the Crown lay in the American South. If they could land enough troops below Chesapeake Bay, the British reasoned, the large amount of Loyalist support would aid a push through the northern colonies.

England's alternate plan in the North consisted of troops taking New York City and dividing the rebel forces along geographical lines along the Hudson River. By advancing upriver while reinforcements pushed down from Canada, the British could take control of the entire Hudson Valley, effectively sealing off New England. Lord Germain, the new British minister of American affairs, favored this plan and began to organize an overwhelming strike.

Britain made its first thrust toward the mouth of the Hudson River in 1776 with nearly 450 ships and some 30,000 soldiers. On orders from Congress, Washington moved to defend New York, but weak numbers and bad terrain made his mission impossible. In the Battle of Long Island, Washington barely escaped having his forces wiped out. Remarkably, the British commander called off a direct attack, allowing Washington's men to slip away.

C. "Victory or Death": A Desperate Gamble Pays Off

After the defeat at the Battle of Long Island, rebel troops retreated south to avoid capture. The British government offered liberal pardons, and looked to end the rebellion without alienating the majority of the American population. Desertions mounted as Washington's army, lacking supplies, faced starvation, biting winter weather, and the end of enlistments. The successful early-morning surprise attack on Hessian troops quartered at Trenton provided the rebels with desperately needed supplies. Without waiting, Washington advanced his army towards Princeton to surprise and defeat Cornwallis' reinforcements. The successes of the New Jersey campaign gave new life to the American army as it took winter quarters at Morristown, New Jersey.

III. The Struggle to Win French Support

A. Breakdown in British Planning

With his army still intact, Washington moved to change conditions in the army. Congress remained concerned about the consequences of having a "standing army," but reluctantly agreed to Washington's request for three-year enlistments, better pay, and greater authority over his troops. In the midst of a slumping economy, many Americans, including immigrants and skilled laborers, volunteered for the cause. All lacked training, supplies, and immunity to smallpox, which ravaged the camps over the winter.

British plans for the 1777 fighting year centered on a complex plan to destroy the American forces in the North. Generals Burgoyne and St. Leger would lead two armies and strike southward from Canada, while Howe's forces would move northward from New York, crushing the rebel forces between them. Howe, certain that his troops would not be needed to ensure a British victory, planned to attack Philadelphia. The two generals never integrated their plans and the results were disastrous.

B. Saratoga Tips the Balance

British delays in getting underway afforded Washington the chance to march south in defense of Philadelphia. But at the Battle of Brandywine, Howe caught Washington by surprise, using the same maneuvers tried at Long Island the year before. The British general succeeded in taking Philadelphia, only to discover that the Congress had escaped. Days later, an American defeat at Germantown closed the campaign season for the year. Washington went into winter quarters at Valley Forge, secretly pleased with the combat experience his troops had endured.

Meanwhile, in the Canadian north, Burgoyne had moved his large army south with small, fast-moving American units under Benedict Arnold falling back before them along the length of Lake Champlain. The British felt that their army was invincible, but as supply lines began to lengthen, valuable time had to be spent cutting new roads through near-virgin forest. Also, reinforcements expected from the west never arrived.

At this time, American strength had grown to 7,000 troops in response to arrogant British rhetoric, and Congress had given the Hudson Valley command to Horatio Gates, a sworn enemy of Benedict Arnold. Burgoyne pushed towards Albany, hoping to find Howe's nonexistent reinforcements. While the British crossed the Hudson at Saratoga, Gates's American forces dug in. Once battle commenced, Horatio Gates refused to send his troops to support Benedict Arnold. Despite these problems within the Continental ranks, determined fighting by the Continentals and the capture of Burgoyne's supply trains forced Burgoyne to surrender 5,800 troops at Saratoga.

C. Forging an Alliance with France

In light of the victory at Saratoga, Benjamin Franklin was able to convince the French government of Louis XVI to recognize the rebel government and support the American cause.

The two parties sealed the deal in a formal treaty, which was approved by Congress in 1778. France promised to renounce all claims to English territory in North America, and Franklin promised that the Americans would help protect French holdings in the Caribbean. The next month, France entered the war against England, adding its enormous wealth and power to the American cause. A year later, Spain joined France against their common enemy, Britain, enlarging the "brush fire" in America to a broader European battlefield.

IV. Legitimate States, a Respectable Military

A. The Articles of Confederation

One month after the Battle of Saratoga, the Continental Congress completed and approved the Articles of Confederation and submitted the document to the individual states for ratification. After four years of debate and negotiation, the states finally voted to accept the Articles in 1781, formally agreeing to a weak confederation where the majority of power resided in the states. According to the Articles, Congress could not collect taxes or regulate trade; it could only requisition funds from the states.

B. Creating State Constitutions

It was then up to the individual states to create their own state constitutions. The 13 states, though diverse, shared practical needs. Each had just done away with a colonial system of government and needed to establish something new, drawing equally upon the unique models of English law and colonial charters. State citizens and lawmakers debated the rights and responsibilities of citizens, what forms of power the state could exercise, and the qualifications required to vote or hold office. As they were created, the most important aspect of these new constitutions was the need for all of them to be written, specific documents that spelled out the invested powers of the states. Additionally, three common threads ran through each one: limited powers of the governor, strengthening of the legislature, and the prevention of government officials holding multiple offices.

C. Tensions in the Military Ranks

As the war continued, local militias combined to form state militias, and the Continental army was more formally organized. Concerns over pay, discipline, tactics, distribution of supplies, election of officers, and privileges of rank were not easily solved, and these discussions mirrored the intense debate that occurred in the political realm. Two basic tensions were at the heart of all these debates. One involved the stresses inherent when educated gentry and citizen soldiers had to combine their social classes to confront a shared enemy. The other involved the new position many members of the upper classes found themselves in during the war, positions often involving military rank systems considered unfair by persons accustomed to privilege. The invisible lines were many and often stepped upon. Debate also flared regarding the basic burdens of warfare, which always seemed to fall upon the shoulders of the poor.

D. Shaping a Diverse Army

Attempts to improve the army continued during the long winter months at Valley Forge, aided by the drilling expertise of the German volunteer officer, Friederich von Stueben. Improved discipline and fighting ability led to improved morale, though supply and pay problems, lack of new recruits, and civilian indifference remained constant frustrations.

Black volunteers served with the northern Continental forces and militia but were not accepted in the South. While most rebel women remained behind caring for homes, farms, businesses, and children, around 20,000 accompanied the rebel forces as cooks, laundresses, nurses, and water-bearers.

E. The War at Sea

As the rebel army was evolving, the American Navy continued to prove a hindrance. Official birth of the navy occurred in late 1775 when the Continental Congress voted to arm two ships to prey on British supply vessels in the Atlantic. However, the overwhelming opinion of the revolutionary leaders was that a navy would only act as a drain on America's resources and provide little real help against the British. Even so, many states created free-standing navies of their own. Massachusetts's state navy was easily routed and destroyed by the British in 1779.

Despite its legendary strength, the British fleet was spread very thin in its war with America as other European powers (France in 1778, Spain in 1779, and Holland in 1780) joined the battle. The English were wary of possible invasion of their homeland as France had a history of bombarding its shores. In all, the American Navy launched more than 50 ships that captured some 200 British vessels. Additionally, thousands of American privateers obtained licenses from Congress to seize enemy ships and keep the spoils.

V. The Long Road to Yorktown

By 1778, Clinton's British forces had made the return march to base in New York City. Frustrated by the previous year's events, Clinton revived the English southern strategy for winning the war, arguing the South's benefits as a producer of staple crops, its sparse population, warm weather, and wide array of Loyalists. He hoped to wage a campaign from the recently acquired colonies of East and West Florida, striking north towards Virginia and beyond. Also hopeful was the South's large population of African American slaves and Indians, whom Clinton saw as potential allies against Washington.

A. Indian Warfare and Frontier Outposts

Because of settler pressures on tribal lands, the majority of the powerful native tribes sided with the British. In the Ohio region, the attempts to maintain peace were destroyed by the murder of several powerful peaceful chiefs during treaty talks, and the massacre of Christianized Indian men, women, and children at the peaceful Moravian mission town of Gnadenhutten. Sioux, Sauk,

Fox, Chippewa, Ottawa, and Miami Indian tribes received British supplies, granted to reward and support their tribal warfare against American settlers.

In New England, those members of the Iroquois Confederation allied with Britain raided frontier settlements. George Rogers Clark organized Rangers who fought Indian-style and secured Kaskaskia, Cahokia, and Vincennes. In 1779, American General John Sullivan led punitive raids against Mohawk, Onondaga, Cayuga, and Seneca villages, destroying 40 settlements, burning crops, and destroying orchards.

B. The Unpredictable War in the South

The Revolutionary War also moved southward beyond the Appalachian Mountains. In 1778, a Patriot group managed to slip down the Mississippi River unnoticed and take the town of Natchez. Living in New Orleans, the Spanish governor of Louisiana kept purposeful neutrality until Spain entered the war in 1779. Then, Spanish forces drove the British from the Mississippi River and seized Mobile and Pensacola, thereby cutting off supplies to Britain's Creek and Cherokee allies.

Britain regained most of the Georgia colony in 1778, and by 1779, it was actively blocking American and French efforts to take the port city of Savannah. In 1780, British troops sailed south, taking Charleston and capturing 5,500 American troops. Loyalist Banastre Tarleton's dragoons clashed with rebel guerrillas throughout the summer. Congress sent Horatio Gates to the area with fresh troops, but his defeat at Camden and hasty retreat back north left the South firmly in British hands. In a more successful rebel action in the southern backcountry, rebel militia surrounded and destroyed over 1,000 Loyalist troops at King's Mountain.

C. The Final Campaign

Nathaniel Greene was then sent south and took charge of rebel forces in North Carolina. During 1780 and 1781, Greene expertly coordinated guerrilla warfare and short confrontations, exhausting British forces in the field with little damage to the small rebel army. British General Cornwallis confidently expected to complete the southern campaign during the summer of 1781 after receiving reinforcements by sea at the Yorktown Peninsula. Instead, the French fleet, which had defeated the British Navy in the Chesapeake, guarded the Bay while 7,800 French troops and 9,000 Americans surrounded their 8,000 opponents. Cornwallis surrendered on October 19, 1781.

D. Winning the Peace

With such a major defeat on the battlefield, Britain agreed to treaty talks. Congress instructed the American treaty commission, headed by Benjamin Franklin, to sign no agreements without French approval. American negotiators, aided by distrust between the French and British negotiators, secured a favorable treaty that recognized American independence, established the Mississippi River as the western border, the Great Lakes and St. Lawrence River as a northern border, and permitted American fishing in Newfoundland's waters. Spain received East and

West Florida. Similar to previous treaties, no European nation interceded on behalf of Native American rights.

Identification

Explain the significance of each of the following:

1. General Philip Schuyler:

2. Green Mountain Boys:

3. General Richard Montgomery:

4. George Washington:

5. General Thomas Gage:

6. Henry Knox:

7. Bunker Hill (Breed's Hill):

8. General William Howe:

9. Dorchester Heights:

10. General Benedict Arnold:

11. Thomas Paine:

12. The Committee of Five:

13. John Locke:

14. The Declaration of Independence:

15. General Henry Clinton:

16. British Northern Strategy:

17. British Southern Strategy:

18. Lord George Germain:

19. Hessians:

20. General "Gentleman Johnny" Burgoyne:

21. "The American Crisis":

22. The Articles of Confederation:

23. The Fort Wilson Riot:

24. General Horatio Gates:

25. Fredrich von Steuben:

26. Molly Pitcher:

27. Bernardo de Galvez:

28. General Charles Cornwallis:

Multiple Choice Questions:

1. The selection of George Washington as Commander of the American Forces was
   A. a sign that slavery would soon be abolished.
   B. agreed to only after a number of heated and divided votes.
   C. to increase the skepticism of African Americans about the Patriot cause.
   D. an insult to Southern plantation owners.
   E. a rejection of alliance with France.
   Page Reference: 204

2. Washington won a crushing victory against the Hessians at the Battle of
   A. Princeton.
   B. Long Island.
   C. Bunker Hill.
   D. Trenton.
   E. Cowpens.
   Page Reference: 213

3. Unlike the British troops, American recruits found themselves susceptible
   to_____ in the camps.
   A. surprise attack
   B. smallpox
   C. scarlet fever
   D. scurvy
   E. All of the above.
   Page Reference: 214

4. The British general _____ planned on invading the American colonies from
   Canada in hopes of dividing them.
   A. Burgoyne
   B. Gates
   C. Arnold
   D. Gage
   E. Howe
   Page Reference: 214

5. American General Horatio Gates accepted the credit for defeating Burgoyne's forces at the
   Battle of
   A. Fort Ticonderoga.
   B. Trenton.
   C. Saratoga.
   D. Cowpens.
   E. None of the above.
   Page Reference: 215

6. After the Declaration of Independence, the first European nation to recognize the new government was
   A. Greece.
   B. Italy.
   C. France.
   D. Spain.
   E. Holland.
   Page Reference: 215

7. Among the most important tensions within the ranks of the American military was
   A. the desire of some soldiers to elect their officers.
   B. Congressional inability to grant military commissions
   C. lack of class divisions.
   D. almost complete absence of European officers
   E. All of the above.
   Page Reference: 220

8. After recognizing American independence, France was joined a year later by _____ who entered the war on the side of France.
   A. Russia
   B. Ireland
   C. Germany
   D. Spain
   E. New Zealand
   Page Reference: 215

9. Most Native Americans in eastern North America
   A. supported the American colonists demand for liberty.
   B. remained loyal to Great Britain.
   C. hated the French and the British more than they disliked colonists.
   D. remained neutral during the Revolutionary War.
   E. welcomed the prospect of further colonial expansion into their territory.
   Page Reference: 223

10. The first constitution approved by the American Continental Congress was called
    A. the Articles of Confederation.
    B. the Iroquois Confederacy.
    C. the Declaration of Independence.
    D. the Peace of Saratoga.
    E. None of the above.
    Page Reference: 232

MAP QUESTION:

Consider Map 7.2, titled "Overview of the Revolutionary War." What conclusions can you draw from this map about the mobility of warfare during this period? What part did geography or water play?

CONNECTING HISTORY

What other American historical connections can you think of on this scale? Why do you think society continues to repeat the mistakes of the past?

INTERPRETING HISTORY

What do the similarities between The Declaration of Independence and the grand jury declaration tell you about the time in which both were written? Had specific ideas traveled large distances in the colonies?

ENVISIONING HISTORY

Analyze Ben Franklin's use of his plain fur cap as part of his plan to impress the leaders of France. Why was it so successful?

THE WIDER WORLD

Discuss what the journey of Tom and Sally Peters says about the plight and possibilities of enslaved African-Americans in the eighteenth century.

Answers to Multiple Choice Questions

1. C
2. D
3. B
4. A
5. C
6. E
7. A
8. D
9. B
10. A

Chapter 8
New Beginnings,
The 1780s

Learning Objectives:

After reading Chapter 8, you should be able to:

1. Explain the problems facing the young nation after the Revolutionary War that had to be solved immediately.
2. Discuss the value of George Washington's leadership.
3. Detail the evolution of the Constitution of the United States.
4. Understand the conflicts in the Mississippi Valley.
5. Analyze the army's role in the government after the war.
6. Discuss who had the right to vote in America during the 1780s and why.
7. Explain the continued presence of the European powers in America after the war.
8. Understand the difficulty involved in ratifying the Constitution.

Time Line

1780
Revolution Army officers are promised half-pay for life by Congress

1781
Articles of Confederation ratified

1783
Treaty of Paris finalized
Society of the Cincinnati founded
Webster's *American Spelling Book*
Americans granted generous southern boundary by British at 31st parallel

1784
Columbia College (later University) chartered in New York
America established trade relations with Russia

1785
Society for the Promotion of the Manumission of Slaves founded
Land Ordinance of 1785

1786
Columbia, South Carolina founded
Ohio Company founded to purchase western lands

1787
Constitutional Convention of 1787 in Philadelphia
Northwest Ordinance of 1787

1788
The Federalist was released to the public

1790
Cincinnati, Ohio founded
Constitution finally ratified by all states

1791
Vermont became fourteenth state

1792
State of Kentucky founded
Columbia River discovered

1796
State of Tennessee founded

Chapter Overview

Greater than the destruction of the Revolutionary War, smallpox left a path of death throughout the continent from Mexico City to New Orleans to the Canadian interior. Losses were greatest among Native Americans, although few groups remained unaffected. In its eight-year course, the virus killed more than 130,000 North Americans.

As the epidemic subsided, immediate problems surfaced that needed the attention of the government. Still undecided was the nebulous question of what to do about lingering traces of the European powers. Britain still controlled much of Canada, and Spain controlled the western reaches of the continent. Russians were intruding on the coastline of Alaska, and some thought the French might reinsert themselves into American affairs.

I. Beating Swords into Plowshares

Victory over the British did nothing to eliminate the many internal conflicts afflicting the new nation. Foreign policy concerns, debtor/creditor conflicts, and trade wars brought the confederated states to the brink of ruin. In the face of all this, delegates from the states met in Philadelphia to craft a new plan of government.

A. Will the Army Seize Control?

After triumph at Yorktown and a quick march to repel lingering British troops from New York City, Washington's army encamped near the Hudson River. Because the war had depleted the American treasury, most of them had not been paid in some time. It occurred to many that disbanding the army's strength might not be a good idea until the government settled their back pay. In 1780, they received a promise from Congress that money was coming. Two years later, the disgruntled officers sent a delegation to Philadelphia to argue their claim.

At that time, Congress was working on a plan to impose a five percent duty on imported goods to generate revenue for the fledgling country to pay off war debts. Veiled threats of military takeovers and coups circulated in the New York camp. Congress finally found the revenue and offered assurances to the army. In April 1783, word came that articles of peace had been signed in France. By June, most of the Continental Army had disbanded.

B. The Society of the Cincinnati

A military coup had been averted. George Washington had pleaded with the army to respect the necessity of civilian control of the military in a democratic society. Thomas Jefferson later praised Washington's words of liberty but still harbored fears that officers of the army might yet dabble in politics. These fears were seemingly realized when General Knox announced the formation of the Society of the Cincinnati. The new association bore the name of the famous Roman statesman and was open only to officers of the Continental Army serving at the end of the war, former officers, and honorary initiates.

Considered no more than a social club by many onlookers, the society lent itself to suspicion through its rites, secrecy, and sizable bank account. Most disturbing was the society's policy of hereditary membership, so that eldest sons could perpetuate the society for years to come. Washington, an automatic member, was persuaded by members of Congress not to take over leadership of the society, which eventually changed some of its more disturbing policies.

C. Renaming the Landscape

To celebrate the new nation, towns and cities were renamed to wipe away the memories of the hated British and begin anew. Parents began giving their newborns the names of honored individual war heroes and foreign supporters of the American struggle.

D. An Independent Culture

New plays and poetry celebrated America's virtues, extolling the heroic contest of war. A new country needed a unique approach to its language. In his *American Spelling Book* (1783), Webster endorsed a simple, straightforward approach to written English that avoided the stilted conventions of the British. The New England schoolteacher and war veteran followed this success with *An American Dictionary of the English Language* (1828) that listed some 5,000 new words, many reflecting Native American or Dutch origin. Webster also lobbied Congress to establish copyright legislature for the safeguarding of intellectual property.

The new land of America itself inspired many artists and intellectuals. Topography, botany, geography, and social theory became major fields of study. A desire to rebuild and improve society led to improvements in jails, assistance to debtors, and establishment of libraries. Some New Yorkers voiced early abolition opinions and Connecticut citizens protested the abuse of liquor. Regardless of the weakness or stability of the government, it was clear that American citizens knew they were no longer part of a European empire but instead lived in a new nation.

II. Competing for Control of the Mississippi Valley

A. Disputed Territory: The Old Southwest

American settlers moved across the mountains into the rich southern lands of Kentucky and Tennessee and to the northern Ohio River drainage. The Spanish government continued to develop its northern frontier of East and West Florida, New Mexico, and the Louisiana territory gained from France. It also debated about how to deal with the American settlers. Should they be encouraged and urged to become valued trading partners and/or Spanish citizens, or should they be driven out of Spanish territory?

B. American Claims and Indian Resistance

Since the United States was little more than a weak confederation of states, it had no effective control of citizens moving westward and did not try to prevent the expansion. State governments, with little money to pay off returning veterans from the war, issued vouchers for the distribution of frontier farmland. Populations west of the Appalachian Mountains grew so quickly that new states like Tennessee and Kentucky soon entered the union.

Strong southern confederacies of Native Americans like the Creek, Cherokee, and Chickamauga soon found themselves under continued pressure from land-hungry settlers and the competing claims of the Spanish. Damaged by the smallpox epidemic and the trials of war, these tribes tried a number of plans to coexist with the thieves of their land. Some tribes responded by naming new leaders with firm European-American ties. Other tribes followed a different approach and practiced guerrilla warfare against the frontier settlers. Strength, however, lay with the vast number of Americans that kept coming from the east.

C. "We Are Now Masters": The Old Northwest

Like their brethren in the South, the Native Americans of the American North had made a gamble and chosen sides with the British during the Revolutionary War. With the ousting of the British and the Treaty of Paris, American settlers lost no time in claiming northern territories that had traditionally belonged to the Indians. Although the English still occupied a few lonely forts on the Canadian border, they were ill-equipped and hardly able to support the Indians of the region who felt betrayed by the results of the war.

American "negotiators" used leverage and downright terrorism to force tribes to enter into treaties. The former colonies began to cede their claims west of the Appalachians to the

Confederation government. However, Connecticut and Virginia held onto several million acres of western land earmarked for compensation of war veterans.

With a growing reserve of land, the Confederation government became more than a figurehead; it became a sovereign ruling body. Thomas Jefferson was tasked with the administration of the new western lands and, before leaving for France to replace an ailing Benjamin Franklin as the American ambassador, he formulated a plan for efficient western land distribution.

This statute became the Land Ordinance of 1785. To avoid the complications inherent in private surveys and the resulting overlap of claims, the ordinance called for a grid of contiguous townships beginning where the Ohio River crossed out of Pennsylvania. Hoping to populate the West with yeoman farmers, Jefferson endorsed selling the western lands in small blocks rather than large spreads that only wealthy land speculators could afford. Jefferson also included provisions and parameters for these yeoman farmers to eventually join together regionally for self-government and statehood. Congress, however, dismissed some of Jefferson's more idealistic proposals and modified the ordinance greatly.

D. The Northwest Ordinance of 1787

The task of officially surveying the lands of the West would take years to complete. Almost immediately, a new law issued from Congress—the Northwest Ordinance of 1787—went further in changing Jefferson's original plans regarding government and administration of the Northwest.

The new ordinance opened up debate on the acceptability of slavery in the new territory and made arrangements to deport fugitive slaves back to the South. It increased property requirements for voting or holding office and also complicated the process of admitting new states to the union. Many members of Congress were also eastern land speculators and it was in their best interests to create a scenario in which the land could be controlled for profit.

III. Debtor and Creditor, Taxpayer and Bondholder

The end of the Revolutionary War ushered in a period of economic slowdown. The split with England had disrupted habitual modes of trade. Merchants were desperate to find new markets for their goods as the money supply shrank. Violent demonstrations across the new country prompted the Congress to hold closed-door sessions to plan a recovery scheme.

A. New Sources of Wealth

Throughout the 1780s, the overall economic theme of America was a desperate search for trade and new markets. Britain had imposed trade restrictions for the Americans with the lucrative British West Indies in the Treaty of Paris. American merchants sent feelers out to the world, establishing trade with Russia and China in 1784, while searching for profit in the African slave trade. Many New England ships took the middle passage to Africa for a cargo of slaves to replace those who had escaped from the Southern rice plantations during the war.

Trade with China increased with time. The soft furs and ginseng roots of the American interior were highly prized by the Chinese who, in return, exported silks, teas, and chinaware. Expeditions up the western coast of the continent established later American claims in the Oregon region.

B. "Tumults in New England"

One of the schemes manufactured by the wealthy involved the buying of state loan certificates for a fraction of their face value. By 1790, relatively few people in the country controlled the debt of the combined states, and eventually these lien holders wanted hard currency in exchange for their certificates. The average citizen was loath to pay more taxes for the loan payoffs, so a national debate began about the wisdom of the individual states printing more money for the relief of farmers and the payment of state debt.

Local skirmishes over debt, credit, and currency had their biggest impact in the Northeast where a generation of merchants had made a lucrative living trading with the British West Indies and supplying visiting Europeans with a vast array of merchandise. Sudden exclusion from the British markets sent New England's economy into a depression. Many citizens declared bankruptcy and watched as their land and livestock were sold at auction.

C. The Massachusetts Regulation

Wealthy merchants controlled the legislature in Massachusetts and had the power to resist the arbitrary printing of additional money to relieve debt (as some states had done, with disastrous results). As in other states, a small minority of the wealthy had bought up most of the securities and public certificates issued during the war at bargain prices. They expected huge profits when their government was solvent enough to pay off these securities in hard currency.

In 1786, the Commonwealth of Massachusetts had levied a heavy tax on its citizens, demanding that it be paid in hard currency. As most of the farmers in the state lacked any such currency, they were forced to resist this tax and take matters into their own hands, "regulating" events as the North Carolina Regulators had done 20 years before. The farmers focused on closing the courts that instigated foreclosures on farms. This Massachusetts Regulation became known as Shays's Rebellion, named for the movement's leader, Daniel Shays. Squashed by a private militia, Shays's Rebellion underscored the argument that many had put forward for a stronger central government.

IV. Drafting a New Constitution

A. Philadelphia: A Gathering of Like-Minded Men

The road to a national constitution began at the plantation of George Washington in 1785, when commissioners from Maryland and Virginia met there to resolve disputed state boundaries along the Potomac River. Encouraged by the progress made to clarify political issues quickly, the commissioners slated a trade meeting for delegates from all states in the hopes of creating healthy dialogue. Although only five states sent delegates to this trade meeting the next year, news of the unrest in the New England states persuaded those attending to call for an extended convention in Philadelphia the following May. This time, Congress lent its approval and authority, making the Philadelphia meeting a full-fledged Constitutional Convention, a closed-door meeting designed to retool the governmental structure of the United States.

James Madison arrived in Philadelphia in 1787 and began composing drafts and lobbying delegates, some of whom came early to attend a secret meeting of the Society of the Cincinnati. On May 25, delegates from seven states had arrived and the convention was called to order by Washington, the delegates' chosen president. After some debate, members agreed the convention should operate behind closed doors with one vote per state. No public discussions or written records of the proceedings were permitted.

Soon, delegates from 12 additional states had joined; only Rhode Island elected not to send representation. All delegates were white males with above-average education and professional occupations. Most of the delegates favored a government empowered to keep revenue flowing through taxation and creditor-friendly fiscal policy. Many from large states believed governmental representation should be allotted in proportional accordance to population rather than by one vote per state.

Also, most believed that the single-house (unicameral) legislature of the Articles of Confederation should be replaced by a two-house (bicameral) system. John Adams had incorporated many of these forward-looking ideas into the Massachusetts constitution, including a system of checks and balances designed to restrict power from any one facet of government. It was to Adams and Madison that many of the delegates looked for a working blueprint of government.

B. Compromise and Consensus

The Philadelphia meeting, which was later dubbed the Constitutional Convention of 1787, lasted the entire summer and highlighted the myriad differences—personal, practical, and philosophical—amongst the delegates. Ultimately, the members were realists who were concerned above all else with producing a government that their respective constituents would approve.

Many times during the 16-week convention, the process of debate and compromise continued to lead these men to a practical consensus that would benefit everyone a little but give absolute power to no one. Governmental structure, voting rights and requirements, and a method for electing the chief executive were some of the issues concerning the group. The resulting system of electoral college nomination was unusual and seemingly too complicated, but it served to compromise all the varied concerns of the delegates and won prompt approval.

C. Questions of Representation

Two hot-button issues threatened to stifle the convention's progress: political representation of citizens and slavery. Specifically, the question of proportionate representation versus the one-state-one-vote viewpoint caused much friction, pitting large states against smaller ones. The plan conceived by Madison outlining a government with three distinct branches came to be known as the Virginia Plan. This plan called for a bicameral legislature with proportional representation in each body. The House of Representatives would be chosen by popular election, the Senate by individual bodies of state legislators.

As Madison's plan obviously favored populous states, small-state delegates proposed an alternative New Jersey Plan built on the existing framework of the Articles of Confederation. The plan called for a continuation of the unicameral system with one vote for each state. To compromise these two plans, the idea of a Senate was retained and fixed at membership of two delegates per state. Membership in the House of Representatives would be determined proportionately by state size to be determined by a national census that would be repeated every ten years. European countries had never tried a census, so a tricky question emerged: should slaves be counted along with free persons in the headcount?

Slaveholding states wanted the counts to be inclusive because that would give their states more representation. The convention finally considered an agreement on a "three-fifths" compromise, which equated every five slaves to three free people in the census.

D. Slavery: The Deepest Dilemma

In late August, the question regarding slavery was still undecided. Planter delegates from the Southern states refused to accept any document that made any attempt to curtail the slave trade, and most delegates refused to challenge these pro-slavery positions, fearful of losing their other compromises. Ultimately, the framers approved a clause that protected the importation of slaves for 20 years and dictated the methods of handling fugitives. The word *slave* never appears in the Constitution.

In September, members finalized the new Constitution and prepared to introduce it to the public. The majority of delegates had objected to the inclusion of the listing of specific freedoms (Bill of Rights) in the document. Although there were a few dissenting votes, the framers used a state roll call for final approval, not a member-based roster. This allowed them to debut the Constitution as a unanimous agreement on September 17, 1787.

V. Ratification and the Bill of Rights

Having created a blueprint for a new form of government, the framers faced the biggest hurdle of winning public acceptance for a document that would change many aspects of their lives.

A. The Campaign for Ratification

The Confederation Congress was taken aback by the results of the Constitutional Convention. Most of its members supposed the delegates would issue recommendations to improve the existing government, not discard it altogether. Not surprisingly, the sitting Congress refused to endorse it but did pass the document along to the states on September 28. In each state assembly, the various convention delegates used any persuasive technique at their disposals to convince their fellow statesmen to vote for ratification. Calling themselves "Federalists," the framers and supporters of the Constitution created the name "Anti-Federalists" for any dissenters. Alexander

Hamilton and James Madison published collected essays in *The Federalist,* where Madison argued the value of diversification in a large country to preserve the opinions and rights of all.

B. Dividing and Conquering the Anti-Federalists

Opponents of the new Constitution found themselves labeled Anti-Federalists and had to argue defensively from the start of the ratification debate. They painted the framers as privileged elites, with few real ties to the needs of the common man. They bemoaned the fate of local political power and truly believed that a state government could be more responsive and supportive to the needs of its citizens compared to a distant national government. A number of indebted people worried that a national government would favor their creditors over their own well-being. These Anti-Federalist supporters were numerous in the countryside.

The Federalists, however, populated the coastal cities near the seats of government and used tactics of persuasion to leverage control of the state ratification assemblies. Approval of the Constitution came in Massachusetts in February 1788, Maryland in April, South Carolina in May, and New Hampshire in June. Other states followed, but several of them prefaced their approval by demanding the addition of a Bill of Rights.

C. Adding a Bill of Rights

James Madison had two distinct motives for agreeing to pen the Bill of Rights. He wanted to ensure his election by Virginia to the House of Representatives and he also wanted to avoid the possibility of discontented states calling for a second Constitutional Convention to reconsider the whole new government.

In compiling the Bill of Rights, Madison tried to reach a compromise between the need to pass a Federalist-dominated Congress without reducing any of the primary rights of citizens. He pushed 12 statements of political rights through Congress as constitutional amendments. In two years, three-fourths of the states ratified ten of these pronouncements and they became the first amendments to the Constitution.

Identification

Explain the significance of each of the following:

1.   The Society of the Cincinnati:

2.   *Columbia:*

3.   Noah Webster:

4.   Jedidiah Morse:

5.   *Notes on the State of Virginia*:

6.   Society for the Promotion of the Manumission of Slaves:

7.   John Adams:

8.   Cumberland Gap:

9.   The 31st parallel:

10.   Yazoo Claim:

11.   Daniel Boone:

12.   Dragging Canoe:

13.   Land Ordinance of 1785:

14.   Northwest Ordinance of 1787:

15.   The Ohio Company:

16.   Scioto Company:

17.   "Rogue Island":

18.   Shays's Rebellion:

19.   Constitutional Convention of 1787:

20. bicameral:

21. "checks and balances":

22. Electoral College:

23. The Virginia Plan:

24. The New Jersey Plan:

25. the "three-fifths" clause:

26. The Bill of Rights:

27. ratification:

28. Anti-Federalists:

29. The First Amendment:

30. The Articles of Confederation:

Multiple Choice Questions:

1. The renegade Cherokee warrior, _____, led a band of guerrilla fighters called the Chicamaugas.
   A. Pontiac
   B. George Walton
   C. Squanto
   D. Alexander McGillivray
   E. Dragging Canoe
   Page Reference: 243

2. The Indian tribes of the Old Southwest included
    A. Cherokee, Chickasaw, Creeks, and Natchez.
    B. Chickasaw, Creeks, Choctaws, and Wisconsin.
    C. Cherokee, Chickasaw, Creeks and Sioux.
    D. Cherokees, Choctaw, Creeks and Chickasaws.
    E. Cherokee, Chickasaw, Creeks, and Blackfoot.
    Page Reference: 243

3. The end of the Revolutionary War brought
    A. increased prosperity for farmers.
    B. widespread economic depression.
    C. more territory for Native American people.
    D. severe limitations on slavery throughout the Southern states.
    E. a new war with France.
    Page Reference: 247

4. The plan for the orderly distribution of land in the Northwest Territory was codified by the
    A. Judiciary Act of 1789.
    B. Constitution of 1789.
    C. Land Ordinance of 1785.
    D. Township Act of 1783.
    E. Proclamation of 1763.
    Page Reference: 244

5. The majority of citizens faced with rising debts
    A. criticized the continued British presence in the West.
    B. resented heavy taxes used to pay interest to debts owned by the rich.
    C. wanted to forbid slavery in the Northwest Territory.
    D. wanted tight credit and a limit to paper money.
    E. believed that if the rich got richer, they would too.
    Page Reference: 250

6. The economic travails of the postwar period led to increased American interest in
    A. the West African slave trade.
    B. land along the Mississippi River.
    C. Canadian farm land.
    D. whaling.
    E. trade with Cuba.
    Page Reference: 248

7. Debt pressures touched off _____ in western Massachusetts.
   A. the Leveler crisis
   B. the Whisky Rebellion
   C. Shays's Rebellion
   D. the Great Uprising
   E. Bacon's Rebellion
   Page Reference: 252

8. The only state that rejected sending delegates to the Constitutional Convention was
   A. New Hampshire.
   B. Massachusetts.
   C. Pennsylvania.
   D. Ohio.
   E. Rhode Island.
   Page Reference: 253

9. The constitutional plan that called for the creation of a bicameral national legislature with proportional representation in both houses was called
   A. the Connecticut Plan.
   B. the Virginia Plan.
   C. the Pennsylvania Plan.
   D. the New Jersey Plan.
   E. the New Hampshire Plan.
   Page Reference: 255

10. Those who feared the centralization of power in the new national government demanded that a(n) _____ be included with the final document.
    A. Bill of Rights.
    B. Petition of Duties.
    C. Anti-Federalist petition.
    D. antislavery statute.
    E. section establishing a federal court system.
    Page Reference: 260

MAP QUESTION:

After studying Map 8.4, discuss how the grid system of survey was successful in populating the Old Northwest. Who were the big winners?

CONNECTING HISTORY

Discuss why the article calls the Electoral College a "ticking time bomb." What steps could be taken to make the electoral process more reflective of the people's wishes?

INTERPRETING HISTORY

Why were the Confederation Congress and General Washington afraid of a military coup after the Treaty of Paris ended the Revolutionary War?

ENVISIONING HISTORY

Explain the role that "Grand Federal Processions" played in building support for the Constitution. Why were they so important?

THE WIDER WORLD

What does the career of John Ledyard say about the attraction the world had for some Americans? How does this contrast with those Americans who wished to isolate themselves from foreign nations and peoples?

Answers to Multiple Choice Questions

1. E
2. D
3. B
4. C
5. B
6. A
7. C
8. E
9. B
10. A

Chapter 9
Revolutionary Legacies,
1789–1803

Learning Objectives:

After reading Chapter 9, you should be able to:

1. Understand the varied political viewpoints that were competing for prominence at this time.
2. Explain the continued dependence on slavery in the American South.
3. Identify and discuss the primary beneficiaries of the new country.
4. Understand that Republican ideology had profound effects on many aspects of America.
5. Discuss the presidency of George Washington and the problems he encountered.
6. Explain the effects of European political decisions on America.

Time Line

1787
Free African Society founded in Philadelphia

1789
The French Revolution began
George Washington assumed presidency of the United States
Judiciary Act of 1789
First U.S. tariff on imported goods

1790
Congress agreed to fund national debt
Naturalization law limited U.S. citizenship to free white persons

1791
Bill of Rights ratified by the states
Congress issued charter to Bank of the United States
Samuel Slater constructed first American cotton-spinning machine

1792
Washington was reelected to a second term
French revolutionaries beheaded the king and began "Reign of Terror"
America restricted membership in the militia to white men
Vindication of the Rights of Women, Mary Wollstonecraft

1793
France and England went to war over territorial claims in Europe and West Indies
Washington issued Neutrality Proclamation
British Navy seized 300 American merchant ships; sailors taken hostage under impressments
Eli Whitney invented the cotton gin

1794
Battle of Fallen Timbers
Whiskey Rebellion
Fall of the Ohio Confederacy
France outlawed practice of slavery

1795
Chief Justice John Jay dispatched to England to negotiate status of British forts in U.S.
Pinckney Treaty, also known as the Treaty of San Lorenzo
U.S. gained Ohio Territory and much of Indiana
Yazoo Act in Georgia

1797
John Adams became second president of the United States
XYZ Affair in France
American-French "Quasi War" began

1798
Alien and Sedition Acts passed by Congress

1800
Convention of 1800
Presidential campaign of 1800

1801
Judiciary Act of 1801
Thomas Jefferson became third president of the United States
Jefferson launched war against Barbary pirates in North Africa
Napoleon gained Louisiana Territory from Spain in secret negotiations

1803
Indiana territory passed "black law" preventing African Americans from testifying in court
Louisiana Purchase and Senate approval
Marbury v. *Madison*

Chapter Overview

With the revolution won and the new Constitution ratified, Americans settled into the long struggle to define themselves and their society. This chapter surveys the competing political visions in the new nation, the difficulties for African Americans in a country that allowed slavery, and the efforts to define just what the legacies of the Revolutionary War were.

I. Competing Political Visions in the New Nation

Under the newly ratified Constitution, the Electoral College unanimously chose George Washington as president in 1789. Congress proposed ten amendments to the Constitution in response to popular demand that personal rights have written guarantees. By 1791, these amendments had been passed by the states. Believing that the existence of parties in England hampered free and open discussion of issues, the Federalists of the First Congress began to solve the problems facing the young nation. By the late 1790s, the supporters of Hamilton (Federalists) and Jefferson (Democratic-Republicans) represented two opposing viewpoints. The Federalists supported a strong central government that supported business and industry, while the Democratic-Republicans supported states' rights and a dependence on the integrity of small farmers to guarantee the freedoms and obligations of a republic.

A. Federalism and Democratic-Republicanism in Action

Diplomatic relations became strained in 1793 at the outbreak of war between England and France when Washington declared United States neutrality. Despite this official position, citizens chose sides. Ambassador Edmund Genet of France attempted to raise American troops for the war, and England boarded over 300 American merchant ships to seize sailors and cargo. Britain also supplied guns and encouragement to native tribes in the Ohio Confederacy who fought to retain their lands.

As secretary of the Treasury, Hamilton developed the First Bank of the United States, modeled after the Bank of England, to fund the national debt and stimulate the economy. Jefferson opposed not only the national bank but all of Hamilton's centralizing proposals aimed at creating financial stability by encouraging industrial growth.

B. Planting the Seeds of Industry

In 1791, New England was fast becoming an industrial region. Samuel Slater arrived from England and built the first American cotton-thread spinning machine. Although the bulk of manufacturing took place in individual households, innovations such as Eli Whitney's cotton gin helped speed production. America's Industrial Revolution was centered along a geographic fault line from New England to Pennsylvania that possessed plenty of falling water for power, capital from wealthy merchants, and a dense population as a resource for labor and consumption. Mining, fishing, and shipbuilding industries thrived. Innovations in transportation spurred faster growth.

C. Echoes of the American Revolution: The Whisky Rebellion

Despite encouraging news about the future of the economy, in 1794, the Washington administration faced violent dissent from Indian nations in the West under the leadership of Little Turtle. That same year, grain farmers and distillers in Pennsylvania refused to pay their federal taxes, prompting Washington to send a detachment of 13,000 troops to squelch this Whiskey Rebellion.

Many of these farmers faced potential foreclosure due to the hard currency policies of Hamilton; money continued to become scarce, and loan repayment demanded hard money. Using techniques from the Revolution, these farmers spent their rage upon the hapless collectors of the whiskey tax. This rebellion and others like it revealed the deep resentment of rural America against the Federalists. Ultimately, the powers and position of the government stood unchanged.

D. Securing Peace Abroad, Suppressing Dissent at Home

In 1795, Chief Justice John Jay traveled to England under the direction of Washington to form a treaty with England. At issue were the lingering British forts in America, American debt still owed to English creditors, British impressments of American sailors and ships, and the rights of individual Americans to trade freely with European combatants in war-time. Pro-British, Chief Justice Jay had difficulty pressuring the English, and the resulting treaty lacked teeth. Another treaty, the Pinckney Treaty of 1795, provided America with Spain's permission to navigate the Mississippi River tax-free for purposes of trade.

An election year, 1796 saw the campaigns of John Adams for the Federalists and Thomas Jefferson for the Democratic-Republican Party (Washington had decided not to run for a third term). Adams's narrow win as president allowed Jefferson to become vice president. For his first act as president, Adams had to deal with the French, who were seizing American merchant vessels in response to America's treaty with England. To open communications, Adams sent a delegation to Paris to negotiate a treaty with France. However, French courtiers to the king (referred to as X, Y, and Z in official communiqués) demanded the arrangement of a $12 million loan for the French government and a $250,000 cash bribe for themselves to speed negotiations. Outraged, Adams called the delegation home.

In 1800, the new ruler of France, Napoleon, signed a treaty with America called the Convention of 1800. This agreement dissolved the French-American alliance created during the American Revolution, provided restitution for the ships seized by the French Navy, and established a permanent peace between the United States and France.

On the domestic scene, a Federalist-dominated Congress pledged to stifle the dissent flowing from the nation's countryside. To put an end to this perceived threat, Congress passed the Alien and Sedition Acts in 1789. These new laws made the process of obtaining citizenship for immigrants much more difficult. Also new was the presidential power to deport or imprison aliens and the worrisome ability of the government to label any dissenters as official traitors.

Although unconstitutional, the Alien and Sedition Acts were upheld by the Federalist Supreme Court. Many politicians and newspaper publishers went to prison. The injustice continued until individual states set the legal precedent of nullifying any federal statute they deemed inappropriate.

II. People of Color: New Freedoms, New Struggles

The late 1700s saw an emerging pattern of Americans using race as a means of categorizing people and distinguishing groups from each other. No group suffered this discrimination more than the African Americans after the war; even free blacks faced an uphill struggle in the efforts to achieve economic independence. Employment options were limited and white prejudice, sanctioned by law, condemned many African Americans to lifelong poverty.

A. Blacks in the North

Between 1790 and 1804, all the Northern states had abolished slavery. Some approached this decision gradually; others repealed the institution in one fell swoop. Although free, these Northern blacks were seen by whites as a threat to the economic well-being of the population. At the state and national level, blacks were not considered citizens. Some states prevented blacks from voting, serving on juries, and moving freely within the state borders.

As slaves, blacks had experienced and mastered a wide array of skills and crafts, but as free people, they found it difficult to live independently. Many jobs connected with government remained closed to them and local guilds refused to license their trade skills. Unable to compete, most blacks worked in laborious, menial jobs. Undaunted, they established their own households and filled them with unique traditions. Independent black churches and communal societies began taking shape.

B. Manumissions in the South

Between 1782 and 1792, more than 10,000 Virginia slaves gained their freedom through a process known as manumission, or the selective release of people from bondage. Some planters had come to believe that the Revolution and freedom were the will of God, and they could not justify the continuation of slavery within this religious scope.

Throughout the South, manumissions increased the free black population dramatically. Providing for manumissions in his will, George Washington arranged craft apprenticeships for younger slaves and pensions for the aged. Virginian Robert Carver granted his freed slaves small plots of land. These, however, were unusual situations; manumission was not a guarantee of freedom for the slaves, as individual state laws were careful to underscore. Some Southern slaves, seeing the example of manumissions around them, took the initiative and freed themselves, running away to the North.

III. Continuity and Change in the West

At the close of the war, some white Americans acted quickly to claim small amounts of new land, and land speculators like the Ohio Company took advantage of the state and national government decision to sell land in large lots. Slavery accompanied westward development, where new plantations emerged from timbered forests through backbreaking effort.

A. Indian Wars in the Great Lakes Region

In the 1790s, many of the Indians settled in the Great Lakes Region were victims of the Revolutionary War that had forced them to move west; some were long-time residents. These various tribes brought aspects of their many cultures to the region. Thousands died in Indian-white frontier battles as a result of the Northwest Ordinance. Beginning in 1790, in response to the stalemate between settlers and the tribes, Washington sent a succession of three military commanders to suppress the rebellious Miami Indian chief, Little Turtle. By 1795, the tribes were forced to cede a vast amount of Indian territory to the United States. The removal of the British as a supporting factor doomed the tribes to subjugation by the Americans.

B. Patterns of Indian Acculturation

Indian tribes differed in the ways they intermixed with whites. While some tribes chose to continue moving west to avoid prolonged contact, many tribes began a process of trading ideas and cultures with the frontier whites.

Liquor consumption—a practice learned from these frontier whites—was a quick path to destruction for many of the tribes. Alcohol became a prized trade item and European culture had long used it for social lubrication and celebration. Conflicts involving liquor consumption and trade became common, prompting the concern and protests of some tribal leaders.

The Five Civilized Tribes of the American Southeast had their hunting grounds systematically depleted by infringing settlers. After the Revolution, some of the tribes appealed to the government for aid, and some took up agriculture or simple production of consumer goods. Even livestock husbandry was gradually accepted as a replacement for the traditional hunting practices of the Cherokee, Chickasaw, Choctaws, Creeks, and Seminoles. A willingness to adapt to the parameters of the European world allowed the Five Tribes to stay in their homelands and retain a great deal of their native cultural identity. In the West, the Spanish met opposition in their attempts, through the founding of California and Texas missions, to Christianize Indian societies and suppress their native cultures.

C. Land Speculation and Slavery

As settlers poured into the trans-Appalachian west after the Revolution, they brought with them guns and liquor—proven ingredients for violence and conflict. Land speculation forced new arrivals to purchase farms at inflated prices. Many European-American immigrants brought African slaves with them on their treks west. For these reasons, the West soon became indistinguishable culturally from the American East. Although slavery was soon abolished in many territories and states of the Old Northwest, blacks still would lack the right to vote or give court testimony against whites.

IV. Shifting Social Identities in the Post-Revolutionary Era

Revolutionary ideas also influenced unexpected areas of white society, like established churches, class privilege, the balance between political power and political responsibility, and power relationships within families. Reformers sought to promote an idealized society. The efforts might have been more effective had the various groups developed a common agenda, or if the citizens agreed on what needed to be fixed.

A. The Search for Common Ground

In this spirit of reform, a number of groups appeared to benefit various causes such as manumission, temperance, legal grievances, and tax resistance. Freed people of color created new churches designated as "African" to denote a connection with a specific cultural heritage that predated the diaspora and enslavement of the black race. Utopian sects began to flourish, with a religious message of inclusiveness and family.

B. Artisan-Politicians and Menial Laborers

Changes also occurred among workingmen. Craftsmen and tradesmen organized in societies that stressed equality and emphasized their revolutionary roots by marching in local celebrations to honor the Declaration of Independence, George Washington, or the Constitution. These organizations developed into quasi-political establishments and used their influence to exclude undesirables from their particular region or swing legislative opinions. The use of wage labor over indentured labor or slavery increased the mobility of male unskilled workers who were unable to find enough work in one location and needed to travel to find sufficient income to provide for their families. While the postwar period provided opportunity for some, the majority of small farmers and wage laborers encountered greater problems.

C. "Republican Mothers" and Other Well-off Women

Some women expecting greater freedom and opportunity in the new nation would be disappointed. Rather than acquiring the right to participate equally in the political sphere, own property, or act as legal persons, women were tied more fully to the patriarchal household and familial responsibilities than during the colonial period because of the new definition of a woman's role within the nation. The concept of "Republican Motherhood" supposedly settled any gender issues among elite and middle-class women by identifying the role of mother as crucial to the creation of Republican sons, who would become the solid citizens that would guarantee the survival of the nation.

D. A Loss of Political Influence: The Fate of Non-elite Women

For the ranks of women in America that could not be considered elite, the Revolution had a very specific impact. Among the Cherokee nation, the traditional role of women as negotiators and policy-makers became subdued after exposure to the male-oriented structure of the European-American culture. By the end of the century, women had no influence in negotiations or land transactions.

Impoverished whites and free black women had little recourse to working at a number of labor-intensive jobs to survive. In short, most women had neither the opportunity nor the resources for economic improvement on any level after the Revolutionary War.

V. The Election of 1800: Revolution or Reversal?

A. The Enigmatic Thomas Jefferson

Many Americans at the turn of the century recognized Jefferson as the writer of the Declaration of Independence, but he was also a staunch advocate of slavery and believed in the scientific superiority of the white race. Although idealistic, his views on private property and Indian relations would pave the way for the destruction of numerous tribal cultures.

B. Protecting and Expanding the National Interest: Jefferson's Administration to 1803

The strongly contested election of 1800 removed the Federalists from control of the presidency, but it did not destroy their influence in the national arena. Federalist designates to the Supreme Court, appointed for life, interpreted the Constitution for the next generation. In *Marbury v. Madison*, the Supreme Court established the judiciary's right to declare acts of both congress and the President as unconstitutional. It would be reasonable to assume that Jefferson's presidential leadership as a Democratic-Republican would significantly alter national direction. However, his narrow margin of victory dictated a more cautious approach.

In international affairs, Jefferson did not take the side of France and embroil the United States in the ongoing European conflicts. The purchase of the Louisiana Territory from France removed a potential threat to America's western boundary and added 828,000 square miles to American territory. The four-year war with the "Barbary States" of North Africa demonstrated the determination of the new nation to protect both United States citizens and foreign trade. He was less successful in getting England and France to respect the sovereignty of American ships.

Identification

Explain the significance of each of the following:

1.   The French Revolution:

2.   George Washington:

3.   The Judiciary Act of 1789:

4.   Alexander Hamilton:

5.   Democratic-Republicans:

6.   John Adams:

7.   Neutrality Proclamation:

8.   Citizen Edmund Genet:

9.   impressments:

10. Bank of the United States:

11. "Report on the Subject of Manufactures" (1791):

12. Eli Whitney:

13. The Lancaster Turnpike:

14. The Battle of Fallen Timbers:

15. The Whiskey Rebellion:

16. John Jay:

17. Pinckney Treaty:

18. XYZ Affair:

19. Quasi War:

20. The Convention of 1800:

21. The Alien and Sedition Acts:

22. mulatto:

23. Free African Society:

24. manumission:

25. Little Turtle:

26. liquor:

27. Handsome Lake:

28. The Five Civilized Tribes of the Southeast:

29. Yazoo Act:

30. The Louisiana Purchase:

Multiple Choice Questions:

1. Alexander Hamilton and his supporters believed that _____ would protect local industries and lead to economic growth.
    A. commercial treaties
    B. regional specialization
    C. income taxes
    D. protective tariffs
    E. free market competition
    Page Reference: 265

2. In 1794, _____ challenged the power of the federal government and underscored class conflicts.
   A. Shays's Rebellion
   B. the Regulators
   C. Bacon's Rebellion
   D. the Burr conspiracy
   E. the Whiskey Rebellion
   Page Reference: 268

3. The 1795 Treaty that was meant to stop hostilities between England and the United States was
   A. the XYZ Affair.
   B. Jay's Treaty.
   C. Pinckney's Treaty.
   D. the Treaty of Paris.
   E. the Treaty of Canada.
   Page Reference: 269

4. The Alien and Sedition Acts passed in 1789 by the Federalist Congress was intended to
   A. expel English Catholics from the United States.
   B. establish immigration quotas for the first time.
   C. suppress a rising chorus of criticism from many Americans of the government.
   D. relocate Indian tribes west of the Mississippi River.
   E. make it easier for immigrants to become citizens.
   Page Reference: 270

5. In the West, many African Americans
   A. were unwelcome and even when free possessed fewer rights than whites.
   B. became wealthy land owners.
   C. "went native" and joined Indian tribes
   D. began to be elected to the House of Representatives.
   E. remained slaves.
   Page Reference: 280

6. The Democratic-Republican congressman, _____, was jailed by the Federalists under the Alien and Sedition Acts.
   A. John Quincy Adams
   B. Mathew Lyon
   C. Henry Knox
   D. James Madison
   E. Patrick Henry
   Page Reference: 270

7. The legal process by which slaves could be freed was called
    A. taxation.
    B. regulation.
    C. liberation.
    D. manumission.
    E. coronation day.
    Page Reference: 273

8. The general who defeated the Ohio Confederacy at Fallen Timbers was
    A. Horatio Gates.
    B. Arthur St. Clair.
    C. Josiah Hamar.
    D. William Harrison.
    E. Anthony Wayne.
    Page Reference: 276

9. The case of *Marbury v Madison* in 1803
    A. upheld the election of President Jefferson in 1800.
    B. forced James Madison to resign as Vice President.
    C. established judicial review allowing courts to find actions and laws unconstitutional.
    D. upheld Aaron Burr's conviction for treason.
    E. forced Thomas Marbury to resign from the Supreme Court.
    Page Reference: 292

10. The Election of 1800 brought _____ to power and ended the Federalist control of the national government.
    A. John Adams
    B. Thomas Jefferson
    C. George Washington
    D. Aaron Burr
    E. James Madison
    Page Reference: 289

MAP QUESTION:

After studying Map 9.3, can you construct a time line that details the order of claims and territorial treaties that extended the borders of the United States to the Mississippi River?

CONNECTING HISTORY

Is the United States government guilty of potential violations of civil liberties today? List and discuss some examples. Are these violations necessary or largely arbitrary?

INTERPRETING HISTORY

Is the traditional participation of organized labor in politics still a factor in today's government? Why or why not?

ENVISIONING HISTORY

In what way were women equal citizens of the new republic? In what ways, were they not? Explain!

THE WIDER WORLD

What does the chart say about early American society? Would a chart look like this today? Why or why not?

Answers to Multiple Choice Questions

1. D
2. E
3. B
4. C
5. A
6. B
7. D
8. E
9. C
10. B

Chapter 10
Defending and Expanding the New Nation,
1803–1818

Learning Objectives:

After reading Chapter 10, you should be able to:

1. Understand the motivations behind America's decision to declare war on Britain in 1812.
2. Explain the dynamics of the war: who fought who and the war's outcome.
3. Discuss the role that Native Americans played in the War of 1812.
4. Analyze the economic effects of the War of 1812.
5. Understand the growth of the agricultural South and the associated growth in slavery.

Time Line

1804
Thomas Jefferson reelected president of United States
Alexander Hamilton killed in duel with Aaron Burr

1805
Battle of Trafalgar
Battle of Austerlitz

1806
Orders in Council passed by English Parliament
Congress authorized building of National Road

1807
Embargo of 1807 on all American exports to the European powers
American vessel *Chesapeake* came under attack
Aaron Burr tried for treason
Robert Fulton unveiled his steamboat, *Clermont*

1808
Prophet's Town founded in Indiana
U.S. officially outlawed importation of new slaves

1809
James Madison became fourth president of the United States
Non-Intercourse Act

1810
Macon's Bill No. 2 passed by Congress
The United Society of Chimney Sweeps, New York City, founded

1811
U.S. campaign against Prophet's Town movement
Charter of Bank of the United States expired

1812
War of 1812 began
U.S. unsuccessfully attacked Canada
British captured Detroit

1813
U.S. defeated British fleet on Lake Erie

1814
British defeated Napoleon
Battle of Chippewa
Battle of Bladensburg, Capitol building and White House burned
The Star Spangled Banner written by Francis Scott Key
Treaty of Horseshoe Bend

1815
Battle of New Orleans, final British defeat of the war
Treaty of Ghent

1816
Tariff of 1816

1817
Rush-Bagot Treaty of 1817

1818
Convention of 1818

Chapter Overview

Just because the British surrendered at Yorktown to end the Revolutionary War did not mean they ceased to be a political and military problem for the United States. In fact, conflicts with England and France led to hostilities with both nations. This chapter also discusses increasing regional economic specialization, especially the transformative effect of the rise of the cotton economy in the South.

I. The British Menace

A. The Embargo of 1807

During the Napoleonic Wars, England sought to control American shipping by continuing the practice of seizing both crewmen and cargo from American merchant ships. In an attempt to force European nations to respect American sovereignty, President Jefferson requested an embargo on all exports to European destinations in 1807. Citizens in both New England and the South compared Jefferson to George III because he refused to lift the embargo that crippled their economies. As a result, privateers risked prosecution by circumventing the embargo, illegally routing goods north through Canada and then to Europe.

B. On the Brink of War

In 1809, newly elected president James Madison and the Congress replaced the embargo that banned shipment to all of Europe with a Non-Intercourse Act that excluded shipments to England and France only. England's continued harassment of American shipping led western congressmen, nicknamed "war hawks," to demand formal war against the British to protect American independence.

Land issues continued to trouble western settlers who broke treaties by settling on Indian land. Shawnee war leader Tecumseh built a coalition of tribes from Florida to Canada based on a vision from the Great Spirit received by holy man Tenskwatawa asking his people to drive the white men from their lands. The governor of Indiana led a U.S. army attack against Prophet's Town, and soundly defeated the army led by Tenskwatawa, who believed that the whites were too weak to beat warriors.

II. The War of 1812

A. Pushing North

By 1812, the western congressmen succeeded in their demands for a war with England to halt the threat to American ships and eliminate Canadian trade with native peoples. The U.S. attack on Canada in 1812, similar to the Revolutionary War experience, failed because militias refused to leave their states. The American Navy won small engagements on the Great Lakes and Lake Champlain. The American attack on Montreal failed, and pursuing British troops burned Fort

Niagara and surrounding towns. In Europe, Britain finally defeated Napoleon, which freed up 15,000 British regulars for the escalating war with America. American victories at Lake Erie and the Battle of Chippewa were not enough to relieve the American posture of defense.

B. Fighting on Many Fronts

As in the Revolutionary War, the majority of native tribes fought for the British because of the actions of land-hungry American settlers. Tecumseh joined the British effort, with the rank of brigadier general. In 1813, the most significant event in the Canadian theater was the death of Tecumseh at the Battle of the Thames. In the South, the Creek nation divided its allegiance between the British and the Americans. Andrew Jackson, with 3,500 troops and Cherokee, Choctaw, Chickasaw, and Creek warriors, wasted Creek villages, forcing the Creeks to cede 23 million acres of their homeland in the Treaty of Horseshoe Bend. Despite evidence of battlefield atrocities, Jackson praised his troops for bringing civilization to the area.

The British Navy controlled the Atlantic Ocean, British armies defeated poorly led and poorly motivated American troops, and all major American port cities were in British hands by 1814, except New Orleans. Andrew Jackson led an army to defend New Orleans, unaware that by the time he had reached the area the war was over. The battle on January 8, 1815, which lasted half an hour, was an astonishing American victory.

C. An Uncertain Victory

American and British negotiators had reached a war-ending peace agreement two weeks before the Battle of New Orleans. However, many veterans later wrongly associated "Old Hickory" Jackson with the decisive victory of the war. President Madison had decided to end the conflict in 1814 and sent an envoy to Ghent, Belgium to start negotiations with the British. Early on, the British insisted on the creation of an American Indian territory in the Great Lakes region as well as the relinquishment of Maine to England. The Americans refused, and negotiations wore on. Meanwhile, New England protested the ongoing drain of "Mr. Madison's war" and provided little aid during the conflict; several states even threatened to secede from the union.

As events wore on, the British sensed their potential defeat in the American theatre and feared new threats from France. In the finalized Treaty of Ghent, they dropped their demands for an Indian buffer state and Maine territory. They also agreed to an armistice that relegated both combatants back to their original boundaries before the war.

III. The "Era of Good Feelings"?

By the time James Monroe became President in 1817, the bitter discord that had been so common in Congress and small-town America seemed to have disappeared. Optimism about the future of the country ran high, and the new president predicted an end to the long-standing Indian troubles. Two new treaties set the U.S.-Canadian border at the 49th parallel and established joint occupancy of the Oregon Territory for ten years.

A. Praise and Respect for Veterans after the War

Veterans of the War of 1812 won the praise of a grateful nation and the grudging respect of the British military. To reward these veterans, Congress approved the distribution of 160-acre plots of land in the territory between Illinois and the Mississippi Rivers. This series of land grants did much to open a new frontier in the United States. Two military heroes would eventually become presidents of the United States—Andrew Jackson in 1824 and William Henry Harrison in 1840.

B. A Thriving Economy

New home industries became stronger as the impact of the embargo and war provided them with customers. Reliance on imports had finally given way to a reliance on those goods produced at home. Internal migration became a commonplace event during this period, with families moving in search of optimal standards of living. Toll roads and steamboats facilitated the movement of people and goods. The interruption of trade with Europe as a result of the embargo and the war resulted in a quick growth of industry throughout the United States. Craftsmen finally did not have to worry about foreign competition.

C. Transformations in the Workplace

In some crafts, like leatherwork, barrel making, newspaper printing, etc., large establishments replaced small shops. Skilled artisans were dismayed, while unskilled workers found steady employment. New England dominated textile production and, faced with a shortage of manpower due to the scarcity of slaves, hired women and children in the mills. There were early attempts at labor unions, complete with parades and small strikes, which neither factory owners nor the courts tolerated. Male and female free blacks did the heaviest and dirtiest jobs for scant wages. Slaves continued to labor at whatever jobs would bring their owners the most money or greatest prestige.

D. The Market Revolution

The rapid economic transformations of the early nineteenth century, called the market revolution, was driven by improvements in transportation, commercialization, and the growth of factories. By the middle of the century, the United States had become a very different place to live. Wage workers replaced family labor and indentured servants as the most important labor system in the North. Both private individuals and public institutions invested the money necessary for these changes. Americans in the North began to think in terms of buying products rather than making them at home. Still, traditional forms of inequality and hierarchy continued, particularly for slaves and hard-pressed Western Indians.

IV. The Rise of the Cotton Plantation Economy

A. Regional Economies of the South

As rich lands opened up in the South, indigo production was replaced by cotton production. The widespread use of the new cotton gin made this staple crop profitable in many areas of the

South's interior. In the low country of coastal South Carolina and Georgia, rice production also flourished with the technical advances of tidal farming and the efficient consolidation of small farms into huge plantations. Despite its state ban on importation of African slaves, the demand for labor so exceeded the supply that South Carolina aggressively reopened the trade in 1803 until the federal government's outlawing of import slavery in 1808.

B. Black Family Life and Labor

As most states depended on the internal slave market due to the 1808 federal ban on importation of new slaves, owners encouraged women to have children, with some owners supporting limited marriage arrangements because it improved the work done on the plantation and decreased the number of runaways. Black families supported each other in both kin and fictive kin arrangements that provided mutual support in raising families and surviving slavery. However, masters showed little inclination to take family into account when they parceled out specialized work assignments to men, women, and children alike; ultimately, slaves were property that could be inherited, sold, or killed at the whim of the white master. Ideally, a slave would find himself or herself at a large, stable plantation where there was little chance of separation from loved ones. Rice plantations were desirable as they usually operated on the task system of labor which afforded many slaves the ability to pursue private endeavors.

C. Resistance to Slavery

As the need for slaves increased, restrictions on slave activity also increased. Owners sought firmer control of slaves' lives, afraid of slave retaliation. Harsh punishments were common, and both active and passive resistance to slavery became normal. Work slowdowns, feigned illnesses, accidental fires, breaking tools, misunderstanding directions, and running away for short periods of time were all common. Most whites understood intuitively that danger lurked behind every situation that included a slave, and the resulting fear may help to explain the colossal punishments and deprivations that were heaped upon these people.

Identification

Explain the significance of each of the following:

1.   The Lewis and Clark Expedition:

2.   The Battle of Trafalgar:

3.   The Battle of Austerlitz:

4.   The Orders in Council:

5. The Embargo of 1807:

6. Aaron Burr:

7. The Non-Intercourse Act:

8. "war hawks":

9. Macon's Bill No. 2:

10. Tecumseh and Tenskwatawa:

11. Prophet's Town:

12. William Henry Harrison:

13. Battle of Tippecanoe:

14. General Isaac Brock:

15. Commodore Oliver Perry:

16. The Battle of Bladensburg:

17. Francis Scott Key:

18. Andrew Jackson:

19. The Red Sticks:

20. Horseshoe Bend:

21.   The Battle of New Orleans:

22.   "Old Hickory":

23.   The Treaty of Ghent:

24.   The Rush-Bagot Treaty of 1817:

25.   The Convention of 1818:

26.   "The Era of Good Feelings":

27.   "The Ridge":

28.   Robert Fulton:

29.   United Society of Chimney Sweeps:

30.   "Nat" and "Jezebel":

Multiple Choice Questions

1.   In the first decade of the nineteenth century, Great Britain upset the U.S. by
        A.   the Treaty of Paris.
        B.   invading Canada.
        C.   selling cannons to the Sioux Indians.
        D.   seizing or impressing American sailors and forcing them to work on British ships.
        E.   refusing to buy American cotton.
        Page Reference: 301

2. The War of 1812 was ended
    A. by the Treaty of Paris.
    B. by the Treaty of Ghent.
    C. by the Battle of New Orleans.
    D. by the Treaty of London.
    E. without a formal treaty being signed.
    Page Reference: 310

3. To thank war veterans for their national service, Congress
    A. invited many officers to Washington for a formal ceremony.
    B. created Veterans' Day.
    C. offered land between the Illinois and Mississippi rivers.
    D. proclaimed a national day of prayer for the fallen.
    E. set aside war bonuses.
    Page Reference: 312

4. Which of the following is true about the early Industrial Revolution?
    A. There was a shortage of adult men willing to work in factories.
    B. Some workers felt the factory system took away their freedom.
    C. African Americans, even when free, were discriminated against.
    D. Women often worked in textile mills.
    E. All of the above.
    Page Reference: 316

5. Thanks to an extensive river system and improved infrastructure, a thriving textile industry sprang up
    A. in New England.
    B. in the Piedmont South.
    C. near Baltimore.
    D. along the Atlantic seaboard.
    E. in the Great Lakes region.
    Page Reference: 315

6. The institution of slavery was redefined in the American South in the early decades of the nineteenth century by the
    A. expansion of the sugar economy in the Caribbean.
    B. growth and spread of the cotton economy.
    C. end of the slave trade in the United States.
    D. order of the federal government.
    E. All of the above.
    Page Reference: 318

7. The South Carolina _____ economy recovered and became increasingly profitable in the first decades of the nineteenth century.
    A. tobacco
    B. indigo
    C. rice
    D. cotton
    E. sugar
    Page Reference: 319

8. The regional economy of south Louisiana emphasized the
    A. fishing industry.
    B. production of colorful dyes.
    C. production of textiles.
    D. production of cotton.
    E. production of sugar.
    Page Reference: 320

9. The increasing demand for slaves in the Old Southwest had a negative impact on
    A. westward migration into the Ohio Valley.
    B. the Caribbean slave trade.
    C. rice production in South Carolina.
    D. the slave family structure.
    E. All of the above.
    Page Reference: 320

10. In the South Carolina low country, slaves spoke a pidgin dialect called
    A. Senegalese.
    B. French Creole.
    C. English.
    D. Ghanian.
    E. Gullah.
    Page Reference: 323

MAP QUESTION:

After studying Map 10.3, consider the political and military importance of the territory controlled by England. Who actually won the war? Did the outcome of the Battle of New Orleans have much actual effect on the outcome of the war?

CONNECTING HISTORY

What are some of the dangers to national transportation today? How could those problems be solved in the future?

INTERPRETING HISTORY

Why was it so crucial at this time for the Cherokee nation to reverse decades of tradition and suddenly exclude women from a role in which they had excelled?

ENVISIONING HISTORY

Discuss the ways some Southwest Indians tried to adapt to the dominance of white America. How are these reflected in the painting?

THE WIDER WORLD

Explain how and why the slave trade continued after the United States outlawed it in 1808.

Answers to Multiple Choice Questions

1. D
2. B
3. C
4. E
5. A
6. B
7. C
8. E
9. D
10. E

Chapter 11
Expanding Westward:
Society and Politics in the "Age of the Common Man,"
1819–1832

Learning Objectives

After reading Chapter 11, you should be able to:

1. Understand Indian relocation policy in the United States during the Jackson Administration.
2. Discuss the special situation of the Cherokee Nation and how it retained its homeland while other tribes were removed.
3. Explain the skewed hierarchy of American society: white men held all political power while women, blacks, and Indians were virtually invisible.
4. Discuss the lure of fertile land in the West and the political problems western settlers faced.
5. Detail the growing incidents of slave revolts and rebellions of this period.
6. Understand the ways western immigrants maintained ties with family and friends "back east."

Time Line

1818
General Andrew Jackson authorized to broaden his assault on the Seminole Indians

1819
United States consisted of 22 states
Territory of Missouri applied for statehood
Panic of 1819
Transcontinental treaty of 1819
McCulloch v. *Maryland*

1820
Missouri Compromise
Land Act of 1820
James Monroe reelected as president

1821
Spain approved petition of Moses Austin to move settlers into southeastern Texas
Cohens v. *Virginia*

1822
Andrew Jackson became first American governor of Florida territory

1823
Monroe Doctrine established

1824
John Quincy Adams elected president of the United States

1828
Andrew Jackson elected president of the United States
The "Tariff of Abominations"
The *Cherokee Phoenix* began publication in Georgia
Sarah Hale became first woman in America to edit a periodical: *Ladies Magazine*

1829
Discovery of gold in Georgia's northern mountains: the "Great Intrusion"
Appeal to the Coloured Citizens of the World, David Walker

1830
Indian Removal Act passed by Congress
Church of Jesus Christ of Latter-Day Saints founded by Joseph Smith

1831
Nat Turner's Revolt

1832
Confessions of Nat Turner, Thomas Gray
President Jackson sent troops to Georgia to begin removal of the Cherokee Nation
Nullification Proclamation
Jackson vetoed renewal of Second Bank of the United States
Bad Axe River incident of the Black Hawk War
Black Hawk and White Cloud surrendered to federal troops

1835
Democracy in America, Alexis de Tocqueville

Chapter Overview

One of the most important political, economic, and social changes in the period of the early Republic was the opening up of the western lands for settlement. This process changed the political dynamics of the young nation and redefined conceptions of democracy. This chapter includes a particularly important discussion of the rise of Andrew Jackson as the symbol of his age.

I. The Politics behind Western Expansion

A. The Missouri Compromise

The right of territories to become states was established by the Northwest Ordinances of 1785 and 1787. In 1819, when the 22 states of the United States were evenly divided between slave and free states, Missouri applied for statehood as a slave state. The heated debate that followed finally ended in compromise in 1820, with Maine admitted as a free state to balance Missouri, and an agreement that in the future slavery above latitude 36' 30' in the Louisiana Territory would be prohibited. Congressmen breathed a sigh of relief, but the Missouri Compromise only delayed the eventual conflict over slavery that was destined to erupt.

B. Ways West: The Erie Canal

Congress encouraged European Americans to push west and south by financing new methods of transportation and sale of cheap land. The number of steamboats on the Mississippi increased dramatically as canals linked western producers with eastern consumers and vice versa. In 1825, the completion of the 363-mile Erie Canal linked the New York cities of Troy and Albany with Buffalo on the tip of Lake Erie.

The canal was a marvel in engineering, financial, and social terms. New York received a vast return on its investment. By making inexpensive manufactured goods accessible to people in rural New York and the Midwest, the canal raised the standard of living. Still, some opposed the changes as destroying traditional communities and bringing in unruly travelers who frequented places selling strong drink.

C. Spreading American Culture—and Slavery

The promise of the West continued to draw settlers to populate new lands. Settlers from the slave states crossed the Appalachian Mountains into Alabama, Arkansas, Louisiana, and Mississippi. The wealthier of these settlers traveled with their human property, intending to establish slavery anywhere they went. New planter elites settled in the area and used slaves to drain swamps, to build levees to control the seasonal flood waters, and to plant and harvest cotton.

Newly independent Mexico granted 200,000 acres in the fertile river bottoms of the Mexican territory of Texas to Moses Austin, who accepted the responsibility of developing the area, bringing settlers who agreed to be law-abiding Mexican citizens.

The Mexican constitution prohibited slavery but supported debt peonage, providing a legal window for white Americans to use slave labor. During the 1820s, Moses's son Stephen Austin brought 1,300 settlers to the region. However, an additional 4,500 uninvited white squatters also moved into Texas. Most of these were genuine settlers who developed the land with the expectation that they would eventually be accepted as citizens by the Mexican government and awarded title to their lands.

D. The Panic of 1819 and the Plight of Western Debtors

In 1819, the Second Bank of the United States required greater financial responsibility from the hundreds of local "wildcat" banks that had extended credit to struggling farmers. Those unable to make regular mortgage payments faced foreclosure, loss of land, equipment, and crops, causing a market scare and subsequent depression known as the Panic of 1819. With fewer crops for the eastern market, food prices skyrocketed. Without the usual volume of trade and access to credit, many small businesses folded. Faced with the reduction in consumer spending and unable to access credit, even the elite plantation owners faced foreclosure.

E. The Monroe Doctrine

James Monroe won reelection in 1820 despite the Panic and depression of 1819. At this time, some of the European powers were claiming land and promoting territorial rights near the American border. Especially worrisome for the government was the Spanish presence on its southern and western borders. In 1818, the president authorized General Andrew Jackson to step up assaults on the Seminole Indian tribe in Florida territory. Suspecting Florida of harboring runaway slaves for the past two years, Jackson used this opportunity to seize the Spanish fort at Pensacola and demand that Spain either suppress the Seminole population or sell the territory of east Florida to the United States. The Transcontinental Treaty of 1819 gave America the Spanish domains of both Florida and the Oregon territory.

Fearful of the devastation that an alliance of the European powers could mean for the United States, President Monroe devised a policy that thrust America forward as a power unto itself. The Monroe Doctrine of 1823 forbade all foreign powers to intervene politically or militarily in the realm of the Western Hemisphere.

F. Andrew Jackson's Rise to Power

The election of 1824 produced no majority in the popular vote, and a close finish in the Electoral College threw the election to the House of Representatives. John Calhoun won the ballot for vice-president and promptly withdrew, changing his support from Andrew Jackson to John Quincy Adams, who the House subsequently elected. The Jackson camp charged Adams with corrupting the electoral process and making sinister deals behind the backs of Americans.

Adams faced Jackson again in the 1828 election, and this time events swung the other way. In an amazingly mean-spirited race, Jackson won a landslide victory. In office, Jackson immediately instigated a national spoils system that rewarded loyal supporters during a president's campaign with administration jobs, while tossing out the preceding president's appointed staff. This practice is still in use today.

II. Federal Authority and Its Opponents

A. Judicial Federalism and the Limits of Law

In a series of landmark cases, Chief Justice John Marshall and the Supreme Court sought to limit the powers of the states within their own boundaries. *McCulloch* v. *Maryland* (1819) supported the Congressional decision to grant the Second Bank of the United States a 20-year charter. The state of Maryland had issued a high tax on the notes issued by the bank; this action was ruled unconstitutional by the Court in the first demonstration of federal judicial review, restated in *Cohens* v. *Virginia* (1821).

In 1832, a case involving the encroaching cotton production into the homelands of the Cherokee Nation in north Georgia aimed the Court on a collision course with President Jackson. The Cherokee Nation had undergone tremendous change in adapting to European ways of life. They did this in hope of retaining their traditional homeland. The discovery of gold in the heart of the Cherokee lands in 1829 led to the "Great Intrusion" of the whites. The Cherokees, who considered themselves a sovereign nation, reached out to the federal government for justice in the face of this veritable invasion, but President Jackson considered the very existence of the Cherokee Nation an affront to his authority. In fact, Jackson favored the removal of the Cherokees to open up the gold fields to unchallenged mining.

With Congressional backing, the Indian Removal Act became law in 1830. This Act provided for the removal of Indians to designated areas west of the Mississippi River. Outraged, the Cherokees refused to sign the removal treaties required by the federal government, and took their case to the U.S. Supreme Court, hoping the Court would uphold the idea of the Cherokees as a sovereign nation. In two decisions, the Court declared Indian nations to be independent of the states in which they were based, but dependent on the government of the United States. President Jackson and the Governor of Georgia ridiculed the Court's presumption of judicial authority. In 1832, Jackson sent federal troops to Georgia to begin forced relocation of the Cherokee people.

B. The Tariff of Abominations

The Tariff of 1828 (the Tariff of Abominations in the South) increased taxes on foreign products and raw material, thereby continuing the "protection" of American industry. Foreign governments retaliated with high tariffs of their own. In the wake of the Panic of 1819, this measure was economically damaging to the South, which had to trade its cotton on the world market to survive. Revived four years later, South Carolina declared the 1832 tariff "null and void" in the state. Jackson rejected the "nullifiers" action as usurping federal power, issued a terse Nullification Proclamation, and proceeded to send troops to force South Carolina to alter its position. Henry Clay, a senator from Kentucky, brokered a compromise and both parties retreated for the time being.

C. The Monster Bank

Andrew Jackson vetoed rechartering the Second Bank of the United States which was due to expire in 1836, claiming that his view of the bank as a tool for the enrichment of the wealthy represented the majority opinion of the nation. Economic chaos followed as local and state banks proliferated. Convinced the bank veto would spell Jackson's political downfall, his opponents seized the issue and pushed Henry Clay into the race for president in 1832.

Clay and his supporters were shocked to learn the Supreme Court had upheld Jackson's veto, stealing much of the thunder from Clay's campaign. Also key was the introduction of an anti-Masonic candidate into the race that further drew away anti-Jackson voters from Clay. Jackson's landslide victory surprised no one.

III. Americans in the "Age of the Common Man"

A. Wards, Workers, and Warriors: Native Americans

In the 1820s, Native Americans, blacks, and women comprised 70 percent of the American population. Consequently, universal white male suffrage provided political power to only one-third of the nation. Political decisions increasingly dehumanized Indians and ridiculed the idea that they had rights that must be respected. The so-called Five Civilized Tribes east of the Mississippi formed their own schools, published newspapers in their native languages, domesticated animals, established farms and plantations, and perfected craft and trade skills that showcased their degree of "civilization." In the Old Northwest, tribes like the Peorias moved in response to increased white pressure on their land. Winnebagos, Sauks, and Fox tribes united under the Sauk chief Black Hawk and clashed with federal troops repeatedly in an unsuccessful attempt to keep tribal lands.

B. Slaves and Free People of Color

The decade of the 1820s saw a natural increase in the slave population of 25 percent, or 500,000 people. The free black population in the North made a similar percent increase, due more to manumissions, while the Southern free-black population increased more slowly. Although the number of free blacks was insignificant, white Southerners feared their lifestyle and attitudes would inspire slave rebellions. The reaction to rumors regarding the freed black man Denmark Vessey in 1822 demonstrated the depth of white fear. These rumors about intended rebellion led to arrests, torture, and eventually the hanging of 35 black men and the exile of 18 others. Witness testimony was contradictory, and historical evidence suggests no reliable proof ever existed that any kind of rebellion was planned.

Nat Turner's Rebellion of 1831, which resulted in the deaths of 60 whites, prompted similar reactions and served to reinforce white fears. Slave owners subsequently implemented policies meant to fully control the slave and free black populations. Northern free blacks also dealt with white suspicions and restrictions on their freedom. Some became active in advocating the end of slavery, a few suggested leaving the country to settle in Africa, some advocated separation from whites, while others urged integration as the best means of protecting themselves and building a future. After the Nat Turner Rebellion a widely read biography of Turner shocked readers in the South. Portrayed as a thoughtful, religious man born and raised under the rule of a kind master, Turner did not fit the stereotype of the dangerous slave. This incident and the resulting hysteria served to solidify the institution of slavery until the American Civil War.

C. Legal and Economic Dependence: The Status of Women

Regardless of what region they lived in, Indian women and slave women had virtually no rights under either U.S. or Spanish law. A white woman also remained subordinate to the law and her husband, having no legal control over property, wages, her children, or herself. She could not make contracts, vote, or serve on a jury. In contrast, a married woman in the Spanish southwest had many more rights.

Few white women worked outside their homes for wages and there were few respectable jobs available, though most made unappreciated contributions to family welfare through housework and child rearing. Well-to-do women redefined their role as managers of servants and the creators of a comfortable home environment for their husbands and children, becoming consumers rather than producers.

In Spanish settlements, women took the responsibility of household production of goods for the family. Indian women had long been traditionally responsible for the efficient operation of the tribe through manual labor.

Though few women worked for actual wages, one exception was in the New England textile mills that were constantly in need of labor due to the scarcity of slaves. Women lived together in boarding houses and followed the strict rules of the company towns.

IV. Ties That Bound a Growing Population

Seeking new opportunities often meant leaving hometowns, families, friends, and the network of one's neighbors. The realm of politics provided one form of continuity for white males. Religion provided many with comforting answers as well as social networks that could fill the need for kin and friends. Increased literacy produced connections through common ideas and imagery. Newspapers, books, and pamphlets also promoted values claiming to represent the best individuals, reinforcing or creating gender roles, defining appropriate family relationships, and providing the rationale for or against slavery.

A. New Visions of Religious Faith

The turbulence of the times produced new methods of expressing religious faith, as chaos usually does. During the Indian Wars of the Old Northwest, a Winnebago prophet named White Cloud joined forces with Sauk Chief Black Hawk to bring together a coalition from several tribes. A medicine man and respected mystic, White Cloud sermonized against the white Americans and encouraged his Indian brethren to take action and defend some aspects of their way of life through submission before it was too late. White Cloud and Black Hawk surrendered together to federal troops in 1832 in an act of spiritual unity against the oppression of whites.

In the Northern states, a Second Great Awakening prompted spiritual revivals and multitudes of new converts. A respected lawyer-turned-clergyman, Charles Finney preached a message of an independent relationship with God buttressed by works through political organizations. In the South, white clerics turned away from their traditional role in the conversion of slaves and looked for the favor of the plantation/well-to-do class of followers. In 1830, Joseph Smith founded what would become The Church of Jesus Christ of Latter-Day Saints.

B. Literate and Cultural Values in America

A former hat maker and amateur writer in Boston blazed new ground for women in 1825 by becoming the first woman in America to edit a periodical. In *Ladies Magazine*, Sarah Hale hoped to better educate American women in the realms of motherhood, piety, and self-sacrifice. Hale and many other women writers believed in the silent, powerful influence women could have on the affairs of the world.

Sentimental poetry and fiction comprised the bulk of literature targeting women in this era. Men, however, began a literary tradition in America of regional histories, landscapes, and heroic struggle. Newspapers, books, and magazines began to flourish, all working to define and describe the quintessential traits of American character. Hard work, attention to family, and adherence to specific core moralistic values were the ideals of Americans as well as the Victorians of England.

Identification

Explain the significance of each of the following:

1. The Missouri Compromise:

2. The Land Act of 1820:

3. coffles:

4. American canal system:

5. Moses and Stephen Austin:

6. The Panic of 1819:

7. "wildcat" banks:

8. Davy Crockett:

9. James Monroe:

10. General Andrew Jackson:

11. The Transcontinental Treaty of 1819:

12. The Russo-American Treaty of 1824:

13. The Monroe Doctrine:

14. John Quincy Adams:

15. Henry Clay's "American System":

16. spoils system:

17. *McCulloch* v. *Maryland* (1819):

18. The "Great Intrusion":

19. The Indian Removal Act:

20. *Cherokee Nation* v. *Georgia* (1831)

21. The "Tariff of Abominations":

22. Nullification Proclamation of 1832:

23. Henry Clay:

24. Alexis de Tocqueville:

25. Sequoyah:

26. Bad Axe River Incident:

27. Denmark Vesey:

28. American Colonization Society:

29. Nat Turner:

30. Joseph Smith:

Multiple Choice Questions

1. The Monroe Doctrine held that the U.S.
    A. had the right to intervene in European affairs.
    B. would not allow foreign nations to intervene in the Western Hemisphere.
    C. would respect the borders of Mexico.
    D. could remove any Cuban government they did not like.
    E. would always ally with France against mutual enemies.
    Page Reference: 338

2. The event that led to the forced removal of the Cherokee from Georgia was
    A. a legal challenge to tribal sovereignty.
    B. the murder of a settler family.
    C. a slave uprising in the Georgia low country.
    D. treaty violations by rum-soaked war parties.
    E. the discovery of gold.
    Page Reference: 341

3. The high tariff rates caused a great controversy in the Southern states and led to the
   A. secession of South Carolina.
   B. expansion of the cotton empire.
   C. collapse of the Second Bank of the United States.
   D. Nullification crisis.
   E. Wall Street panic of 1819.
   Page Reference: 343

4. The politician who sought to exploit the discontent raised by Jackson's veto of the bank bill was
   A. Henry Clay.
   B. John C. Calhoun.
   C. William Wirt.
   D. Daniel Webster.
   E. Martin Van Buren.
   Page Reference: 343

5. The Cherokee responsible for crafting the famous syllabary was
   A. William Holland Thomas.
   B. Broken Arrow.
   C. Sequoyah.
   D. John Ross.
   E. Dragging Canoe.
   Page Reference: 345

6. The African American carpenter who was arrested and executed for plotting a rebellion in Charleston in 1822 was
   A. Gabriel Prosser.
   B. Nat Turner.
   C. Frederick Douglass.
   D. Denmark Vesey.
   E. Osceola.
   Page Reference: 346

7. Nat Turner, a slave preacher,
   A. pleaded for free African American expansion into Texas.
   B. led a slave revolt in Virginia in 1831.
   C. fled to Canada and became a spokesman for the anti-slavery cause.
   D. told slaves to be thankful for having work and kind masters.
   E. argued for an American conquest of Cuba.
   Page Reference: 347

8. Enslaved and Indian women had_____ legal rights in the U.S.
   A. almost equal
   B. a few but very important
   C. completely equal
   D. more
   E. almost no
   Page Reference: 348

9. One of the major leaders in the spread of religious enthusiasm of the Second Great Awakening was
   A. Joseph Smith.
   B. Henry Ward Beecher.
   C. Charles Grandison Finney.
   D. William Lloyd Garrison.
   E. Rev. Billy Sunday.
   Page Reference: 353

10. The author of *The Last of the Mohicans* was
    A. James Fenimore Cooper.
    B. Henry David Thoreau.
    C. Washington Irving.
    D. Herman Melville.
    E. John Greenleaf Whitter.
    Page Reference: 355

MAP QUESTION:

After studying Map 11.3, explain why the intricate system of canals was built in the northern United States and not in the South.

CONNECTING HISTORY

In your opinion, why has the United States allowed the communist regime of Fidel Castro to continue in Cuba, even after the breakup of the Soviet Union? Should the Monroe Doctrine apply in this case?

INTERPRETING HISTORY

Why does the author feel the *partido* way of tending sheep to be so rewarding? Why would a system like this not work everywhere in the United States regardless of the product?

ENVISIONING HISTORY

What is your interpretation of the significance of the presidential inauguration of Andrew Jackson?

THE WIDER WORLD

What does the ever growing demand for cotton say about the world's economy in the first half of the nineteenth century? Explain.

Answers to Multiple Choice Questions

1. B
2. E
3. D
4. A
5. C
6. D
7. B
8. E
9. C
10. A

Chapter 12
Peoples in Motion,
1832–1848

Learning Objectives:

After reading Chapter 12, you should be able to:

1. Explain the reasons the United States went to war with Mexico.
2. Understand why there was less support for the rights of women in the South.
3. Discuss the impact of the various American reform movements on the country.
4. Analyze the movement of slavery into newly developed territories of the West.
5. Understand the impact of the end of legal slavery to the plantation aristocracy in the South.
6. Discuss America's solution to the Native American problem.
7. Explain the major political divisions in American society.
8. Analyze the American utopian movement and its causes.

Time Line

1825
Utopian settlements of New Harmony and Nashoba founded

1829
Mexico abolished slavery

1831
The Liberator launched in Boston by William Lloyd Garrison

1832
Treaty of Payne's Landing

1833
American Anti-Slavery Society founded

1834
National Trades Union founded

1835
President Andrew Jackson guaranteed safety and comfort of Cherokee Nation during removal

1836
Martin Van Buren became president of the United States
Siege of the Alamo: San Antonio, Texas

1837
Panic of 1837
Mt. Holyoke and Oberlin colleges founded, accepted women
Sam Houston became president of the Republic of Texas

1838
General Winfield Scott began rounding up members of the Cherokee Nation for removal

1839
Spanish ship *Amistad* illegally tried to import Africans into United States

1840
William Henry Harrison became president of the United States
John Tyler replaced Harrison, who died after less than one month in office

1843
"Great Migration" to Oregon

1844
Mormon founder Joseph Smith and brother Hyrum lynched in Carthage, Illinois
Modern telegraph invented by Samuel Morse
James Polk became president of the Unites States

1845
Narrative of the Life of Fredrick Douglass, eponymous
Texas granted statehood

1846
Great Britain repealed Corn Laws, opened country to American grain exports
America and England reached compromise on Oregon territory
U.S.-Mexican War began
Wilmot Proviso created regarding slavery in former Mexican territories

1847
New Mormon leader Brigham Young led his church west to Salt Lake City, Utah
Mexico City surrendered, ending U.S.-Mexican War

1848
European uprisings in France, Germany, and Italy
Failed uprising in Prussia
Oneida Community founded
Civil Disobedience, Henry David Thoreau

1849
Know-Nothing Party founded

Chapter Overview

By the 1830s, the United States was a society on the move and under pressure. People from throughout Europe were flooding American shores and settlers continued their westward movement. Social change contributed to social ills and many citizens became involved in reform movements ranging from abolitionism to education reform. At the same time, America's foreign policy became increasingly aggressive. Many believed that it was our "manifest destiny" to spread from "sea to shining sea." Expansion, however, was not without its costs and as occurs so often in U.S. history, those costs exposed racial and ethnic tensions.

I. Mass Migrations

A. Newcomers from Western Europe

European immigrants' experiences varied as they entered the large cities of America. The motivations and destinations of the immigrants depended on their economic situation and the help of supportive enclaves of established immigrants from their home area. In the 1840s and 1850s, over 4.5 million poverty-stricken Irish immigrants fled the potato famine in Ireland. Arriving in America with nothing, these immigrants could rarely move beyond their port of debarkation.

Political instability in Europe increased the number of German families immigrating to America. Some moved inland and bought farms or started businesses. Others might work temporarily for an established fellow countryman, gaining experience, learning English, and earning money to buy land. Starting a business or, if a woman, providing her own dowry for marriage, were common financial aspirations of the newcomers.

In the East, some joined countrymen to form close-knit communities that built schools, churches, and aid societies. Others chose, or were compelled, to join highly mixed communities that encouraged mutual cooperation, the blending of customs, and the sheathing of old ethnic animosities. Some Americans continued to move west, hoping to take advantage of distant opportunities, and to remake themselves in a new environment.

B. The Slave Trade

Demand for slaves and the restriction on importing slaves since 1808 caused prices to quadruple between 1800 and 1860. One out of every ten slave children born in the Upper South was sold to western planters, with the majority never seeing their families again. This internal slave trade made fortunes for a few and paid the basic bills for plantation owners whose crops had not sold well or whose spending habits outreached their ability to meet their obligations. Traders shipped slaves down the Mississippi on riverboats, or chained slaves together in slow-moving coffles and force-marched men, women, and children to distant markets like New Orleans, Natchez, Charleston, or Savannah.

Black Southerners, who moved north, whether they were runaways or free blacks, lived in neighborhoods of their own race where they would easily blend in. Many new immigrants and working-class whites resented the black competition for both skilled and unskilled jobs. Some elite and middle-class northern whites joined abolition societies and worked to keep runaways out of the hands of slave catchers.

C. Trail of Tears

Throughout the 1830s, the American government followed a policy of Indian removal from their traditional lands to pre-structured "Indian territories" in the Great Plains. The Florida Seminoles were ejected as a result of the Treaty of Payne's Landing (1832), which promised the tribe money, blankets, and dresses for the women. The Choctaws, Chickasaws, and Creeks met similar fates. Most Seminoles began the trek west three years later, but a determined few retreated deep into the Everglades to terrorize American troops for the next seven years.

The proposed removal of the Cherokee Nation also produced intense resistance. U.S. troops gathered the Indians into concentration camps before herding them westward in 1838. Of 16,000 natives beginning the journey, 4,000 died on the way from malnutrition and disease while soldiers systematically destroyed all physical remains of the ancient Cherokee culture in the South. The American government expressed its sympathy and respect for the natives during the removal, but the reality was a reversal of every point of agreement entered into between the two peoples. Many government agents became rich by selling food supplies and clothing intended for the Cherokees' forced march.

D. Migrants in the West

Few groups faced as much united opposition from Protestant neighbors and few went as far west as the Mormons who settled in the Salt Lake Valley of Utah. The Mormons had been founded by Joseph Smith in New York State and had quickly moved to Nauvoo, Illinois. Here, the church's unusual tenets of faith and self-supported militia made the local neighbors suspicious and nervous. Finally, civil authorities levied trumped-up charges upon Joseph Smith and his brother Hyram, who were arrested, taken from jail, and lynched by a mob in 1844. Three years later, church leader Brigham Young pulled out of Illinois and led his followers across the plains to Utah. A number of religious groups traveled west to form new communities where they could practice their religion unmolested. A few couples, like the Whitmans and Spauldings, traveled west to build Indian missions and encouraged settlement of the Oregon territories. The Protestant missions had even less success inducing tribal members to change their religion than the Spanish priests who had worked in New Mexico.

E. Government-Sponsored Exploration

The Lewis and Clark expedition of 1804-1806 was the forerunner to many other government-sponsored efforts to make maps and scientific discoveries. The South Seas Exploring Expedition of 1838, led by Lt. Charles Wilkes, lasted four years and ranged over 87,000 miles. Wilkes's arrogance angered many foreign people he met and Fiji Islanders killed two of his men. In response, Wilkes systematically murdered island leaders.

Still, Wilkes's expedition produced lasting scientific discoveries and the samples gathered formed the basis of the Smithsonian Institution established by Congress in 1846. Another expedition, led by John Charles Fremont in 1833-1844, surveyed the Northwest and helped the migrants who later settled there. His final report was of great practical value for people moving west as it mapped the way and gave information about pasture, water, and climate.

F. The Oregon Trial

Beginning in 1834, Protestant missionaries settled Oregon and found themselves in the midst of hostile Native Americans. In 1843, 1,000 migrants arrived in Oregon, starting the Great Migration. "Oregon Fever" was spread by missionaries and government officials in the economically depressed Midwest, which was still reeling from the Panic of 1837. The Oregon Trail was 2,000 miles long and wagon trains took four to six months to complete the journey. Plains Indians resented the wagon trains, which they believed were another group ready to take their land. By 1869, 50,000 people took the trail to Oregon.

G. New Places, New Identities

Many different cultures came together in the border towns where America met Spanish territory, causing some to question the relevance of race and skin color. Mingling of the traditional races ultimately produced households of widely blended cultures or religions. Migration to the West might mean a new identity or new racial assignment altogether. Blacks of lighter skin found they could qualify as white in the West.

H. Changes in the Southern Plains

Plains Indians saw their life transformed by the introduction of horses by the Spanish in the sixteenth century. By the early 1800s, the Comanche, Kiowa, as well as the Cheyenne and Arapaho, had a large-scale trading empire with the horse both a method of transportation and a type of currency. The ecology was changed by the growing horse population as social change hit the Native Americans and new status distinctions emerged, with a small number of wealthy people dominating trade and leadership. As the Bison dwindled, partly because of the growth of horse populations, hardship hit the Plains Indians. By the 1860s, the Comanche population had fallen to only a quarter of what it had been in the 1820s.

II. A Multitude of Voices in the National Political Arena

As the population of the United States became more diverse, tensions emerged between various groups as specific interests sought to communicate their unique messages. American political parties refused to tackle explosive issues like slavery head-on, frustrating the bulk of Americans.

A. Whigs, Workers, and the Panic of 1837

In 1836 Andrew Jackson's vice president, Martin Van Buren, took over the reigns of American government. The Jackson-haters, personified by Henry Clay, formed a political party called the Whigs. In the cities of the Northeast, political candidates from all parties were beginning to pay close attention to the formation of trade union movement.

The factory system had threatened a number of the traditional skilled trades. Tradesmen, seeking protection, joined forces to advance the interests of these skilled workers. Higher pay rates, payment in hard currency, abolition of debtor's prisons, and a ten-hour workday were some of the reforms they sought through the establishment of the National Trades Union in 1834 to support strikes and organize the efforts of some fifty individual trade groups. A long struggle for political recognition lay ahead.

An economic depression—the Panic of 1837—was fueled by eager speculation in economic futures and finalized by a crop failure in the West. Cancellation of loans by the British and soaring unemployment caused this depression to continue until the early 1840s.

B. Suppression of Antislavery Sentiment

A radical voice energized the abolition movement when William Lloyd Garrison began publishing his new paper, *The Liberator*, providing a voice for those demanding black freedom immediately. A new, well-organized society that included blacks and whites, the American Anti-Slavery Society also vigorously campaigned against slavery in the midst of general indifference on the issue. Former slaves like William and Ellen Craft and Frederick Douglass joined free black leaders like Henry Garland and Charles Redmond and white former slave-owners Sarah and Angelina Grimke on speaking tours that vividly brought slavery to life for interested northern audiences.

The majority of northern Congressmen joined southern Congressmen to pass a gag rule to prevent antislavery petitions from being read or entered into the public record. Pro-slavery mobs attacked black schools, publicly threatened and humiliated Garrison, closed down presses, and harassed black laborers. Immigrants continued to make the connection between blacks with jobs and whites without jobs, and continued to support rioting in New York City, Philadelphia, and Cincinnati.

C. Nativists as a Political Force

The American Republican Party, labeled "Know-Nothings" by their enemies, represented the anti-immigrant voters, a much stronger political group than the abolitionists. Found throughout the Northeast and Old Northwest, these citizens were concerned about the impact of immigrants on jobs, housing, religion, and culture. They objected to immigrants working for lower wages, participating as voters or candidates in elections, and building churches, schools, or private clubs.

Anti-Catholic sentiment helped to justify territorial expansion. Many Protestant citizens of America (a majority) firmly believed in the right of their country to seize the land of the papist Spanish. In the large cities, Catholics and Protestants brawled in the streets.

III. Reform Impulses

A. Public Education

During the mid-1800s, crusaders looked at American society and found much that needed attention. Though committed and energetic, no ideology or plan united the reformers. Northern education advocates sought to create schools with similar programs so that children in mobile American families could fit smoothly into their classes wherever they went. Some viewed universal education as the key to uniting the country, making immigrant children good Americans, and teaching such American values as hard work, punctuality, and sobriety. Local school boards remained in control of their schools, resisting the demands of education reformers for universal standards. School boards hired less expensive unmarried female teachers (since women were naturally nurturing), selected the books, and established the criteria for student behavior. More immigrant and native-born northern white children received public education than southern white children. Few blacks had access to education. Unintentionally, the education effort actually increased class differences.

B. Alternative Visions of Social Life

A small number of reform groups tried to reorganize the family, change attitudes toward private property, or alter the wage labor system. Similar to the intentions of the early Puritan societies, utopian societies like New Harmony, Nashoba, or Oneida sought to create ideal societies that would become national models for solving modern problems. Other reformers joined the temperance movement, which sought to alter drinking habits by reforming drunkards or closing bars. Others advocated improving women's rights, though this topic faced internal dissension over what rights should take priority.

There was fairly widespread northern and southern support for married women's property laws to prevent husbands from squandering property and assets brought into the marriage by wives. There was much less enthusiasm for securing the vote, and the issue of abolition drove most southern supporters out of the slowly growing women's rights movement, even as it galvanized others who saw too many resemblances between life under slavery and the treatment of women. As the fight for abolition gained support, the need to end slavery replaced the fight for women's rights.

C. Networks of Reformers

Many reformers advocated multiple reforms. Many women's rights advocates supported temperance. Dorothea Dix led a reform effort to change how the mentally ill were treated. This campaign was supported by people like Senator Charles Sumner, an abolitionist, and Horace Mann, the leader behind the common school system. It was common for abolitionists and women's rights advocates to overlap, as many women compared their situation to that of slaves.

Margaret Fuller was involved in many reform movements, writing about the plight of slaves, Indians, and imprisoned women.

IV. The United States Extends Its Reach

A. The Lone Star Republic

Mexican concerns about the growing number of uninvited Americans in Texas reached a climax when a few influential Tejanos and Texans declared independence in 1836. The Mexican army, led north by President Santa Anna, defeated a small force of rebels at the Alamo, the Spanish mission in San Antonio. Two months later, the rebels defeated the Mexican army, captured Santa Anna, and declared a new nation, the Republic of Texas, making it the only Mexican state to successfully rebel. Sam Houston became the Republic's first president in 1837. Texas independence worried the abolitionist movement; although Mexico had abolished slavery, the new Texas constitution heartily endorsed the practice.

B. The Election of 1844

American interest in expanding westward included the Republic of Texas and Oregon. During the 1844 presidential election, the Democrats promoted James K. Polk with the campaign slogans "Reannexation of Texas" and "54'40" or fight." Both Democrats and Whigs worked to avoid the looming slavery question despite the presence of the Liberty Party and its outspoken candidate, William Lloyd Garrison. Polk chose diplomacy rather than war with Britain over the issue of control of the Oregon Territory, negotiating for one-half of the claimed territory, with the 49th parallel being the mutually undefended border between Canada and the United States.

C. War with Mexico

One of the last decisions of the incumbent president Tyler was the admittance of Texas to U.S. statehood in December 1845, despite the clear warnings from Mexico that any attempt by the U.S. to annex Texas meant war. The boundary between Mexico and the United States remained undefined. Diplomatic overtures to purchase California and New Mexico were rejected by the Mexicans. War broke out in January 1846.

Not all Americans were in support of the war with Mexico, which some saw as an unabashed land grab; others worried about the subsequent influx of Catholics and Spaniards if the U.S. annexed all of Mexico. Abolitionists also objected to the war. In the Wilmot Proviso, an amendment attached to a congressional bill appropriating money for the war, legislative abolitionists declared that no slavery of any sort would exist in whatever lands America acquired from Mexico as a result of the war. In 1847, Mexico City surrendered, and the war ended. Mexico had been no match for superior American military might. The Treaty of Guadalupe Hidalgo (1848) forced Mexico to give up its claim to Texas, New Mexico, and California.

Identification

Explain the significance of each of the following:

1. Ireland:

2. "The Hub of Gaelic America":

3. Diasporas:

4. Revolutions of 1848:

5. Fredrick Douglass:

6. The Treaty of Payne's Landing (1832):

7. Oklahoma:

8. The Second Seminole War:

9. General Winfield Scott:

10. The *Cherokee Phoenix*:

11. Joseph Smith:

12. Salt Lake City:

13. The "Great Migration" of 1843:

14. John Charles Fremont:

15.   Tejanos:

16.   Martin Van Buren:

17.   The National Trades Union:

18.   The Panic of 1837:

19.   William Lloyd Garrison:

20.   The American Anti-Slavery Society:

21.   "Irish confetti":

22.   William Henry Harrison:

23.   *Amistad*:

24.   Samuel Morse:

25.   The Know-Nothings:

26.   public education:

27.   New Harmony:

28.   British Corn Laws:

29.   Sam Houston:

30.   The Wilmot Proviso:

Multiple Choice Questions:

1. The Boston journalist who launched the antislavery newspaper, the *Liberator*, was
    A. Charles Lenox Remond.
    B. William Lloyd Garrison.
    C. David Walker.
    D. Frederick Douglass.
    E. Sojournor Truth.
    Page Reference: 376

2. The South Seas Exploring Expedition of 1838 was led by
    A. Lewis and Clark.
    B. Henry Ward Beecher.
    C. William Lloyd Garrison.
    D. Charles Wilkes.
    E. William Henry Harrison.
    Page Reference: 368

3. The Whig presidential candidate who went by the nickname, "Old Tippecanoe," was
    A. Henry Clay.
    B. Andrew Jackson.
    C. John Quincy Adams.
    D. Martin Van Buren.
    E. William Henry Harrison.
    Page Reference: 376

4. The Panic of 1837 had the effect of
    A. ultimately destroying the National Trades Union.
    B. stimulating the sale of particularly large western grain crops.
    C. causing the passage of the Sherman Anti-Trust Act.
    D. improving wages for most working people.
    E. preventing business failure.
    Page Reference: 375

5. The anti-Catholic American party was also known as the
    A. Liberty party.
    B. Free Soil party.
    C. Know-Nothings.
    D. Whig party.
    E. Republican Party.
    Page Reference: 379

6. In the South, education for slave children
   A. became far more extensive than in the North.
   B. was forbidden by law.
   C. developed a system of separate but equal school systems.
   D. was organized by Noah Webster.
   E. consisted by largely reading and writing.
   Page Reference: 381

7. Scottish industrialist/socialist Robert Owens's experiment in "cooperative labor" was called
   A. Oneida Community.
   B. Nashoba.
   C. Utopia.
   D. New Harmony.
   E. Seneca Falls.
   Page Reference: 382

8. Those New England intellectuals who believed in the primacy of the spirit and the essential harmony between people and the natural world were called the
   A. Oneida Community.
   B. Owenites.
   C. Transcendentalists.
   D. Shakers.
   E. Harmonists.
   Page Reference: 384

9. The president of the newly formed Republic of Texas was
   A. Santa Anna.
   B. Sam Houston.
   C. Davy Crockett.
   D. Stephen Austin.
   E. Jim Bowy.
   Page Reference: 385

10. _____ condemned the U.S. war with Mexico as an "act of aggression."
    A. President Polk
    B. John Austin
    C. Sam Houston
    D. Zachary Taylor
    E. Abraham Lincoln
    Page Reference: 388

MAP QUESTION:

After studying Map 12.3, consider why the government of the United States set aside the particular land that it did for the relocation of the Native Americans. Why that particular area?

ENVISIONING HISTORY

What does this runaway slave ad say about the way owners looked upon their slaves? Explain!

THE WIDER WORLD

Discuss the importance of railroads for the development of the United States. Why was the U.S. ahead of many other nations in terms of railroad track laid?

INTERPRETING HISTORY

Imagine that you are tasked with presenting the opposing side to Senator Calhoun's remarks. What ideas would your argument use?

Answers to Multiple Choice Questions

1. B
2. D
3. E
4. A
5. C
6. B
7. D
8. C
9. B
10. E

Chapter 13
The Crisis Over Slavery,
1848–1860

Learning Objectives:

After reading Chapter 13, you should be able to:

1. Understand how the United States was a collection of regional economies in the 1850s.
2. Explain the ethnic and economic diversity of people in the Midwest.
3. Discuss the northern ideology of "Free Labor."
4. Contrast ideologies of social inferiority with the belief in individualism.
5. Detail the paradox of southern political power and how it promoted the destruction of the political party system.
6. Explain the rise of the Republican alliance in the North.
7. Discuss the ever-deepening conflict over slavery.
8. Understand the significance of Harpers Ferry and the presidential election of 1860.

Time Line

1848
United States defeated Mexico and took over 500,000 square miles of territory
Gold discovered in California

1850
Compromise of 1850 on slavery

1852
American party (Nativists) formed

1854
Kansas-Nebraska Act

1857
Dred Scott decision by Supreme Court

1858
Lincoln-Douglas debates in Illinois

1859
John Brown attacked Harpers Ferry arsenal in attempt to spark slave uprising

1860
Lincoln elected president
South Carolina seceded from the Union

Chapter Overview

California, which had been seized from Mexico, reneged on the promise to give Mexican residents equal rights. At the 1849 California Constitutional Convention, the delegates limited voting to whites and prohibited Indians and blacks from testifying against whites in court.

Indians were reduced to the status of indentured servants and called "lazy" and "uncivilized." Blacks were often kept (illegally) as slaves or arrested and sent to the South for re-enslavement. Workers originally imported from China were used as forced labor and later discriminatory laws pushed many of them out of mining.

Women were a relatively small part of the population in the West and so used this scarcity to gain more power.

I. Regional Economies and Conflicts

In the 1850s, the United States was a collection of regional economies with distinctive physical landscapes, mixes of peoples, and different labor systems. The emerging national economy was being molded by new transportation (railroads), manufacturing (factories), and machines (farm equipment).

The development from regional economies to a national economy pushed the country toward national growth and economic interdependence, while the social/political conflict over slavery pushed it towards civil war.

A. Native American Economies Transformed

By the 1850s, the U.S. had signed treaties with the Plains Indians that enabled European Americans to push westward without fear of attack. Despite their promises, European Americans overran Indian lands without regard for treaties.

B. Land Conflicts in the Southwest

A large number of Mexicans continued to live in lands taken from Mexico. This caused fear that Spanish-speaking people would dominate any new states admitted to the Union from this area; therefore the new territories did not become states until the twentieth century.

European Americans were in conflict with Tejanos over land in Texas. In the resulting battle, they were able to monopolize political institutions, although Tejanos retained much cultural influence.

In the California of the 1850s, authorities battled Mexican social bandits like Juan Cortina, who raided European American settlements and fought Robert E. Lee in the years before the Civil War.

C. Ethnic and Economic Diversity in the Midwest

The northern portions of Ohio, Indiana, Illinois, and all of Michigan, Wisconsin, and Minnesota made up a "Yankee strip," while Germans, Belgians, and Swiss resided in Wisconsin and Scandinavians in Minnesota.

The lower Midwest—southern Ohio, Indiana and Illinois—had strong cultural ties to the southern states. Since many residents of these areas originated in the South, many supported the institution of slavery. In 1851, the Indiana Constitution prohibited blacks from entering the state, making contracts with whites, voting, or testifying in trials involving whites.

Most rural Midwesterners were involved in traditional systems of agriculture. By the mid-nineteenth century, family farmers became increasingly dependent on expensive machinery and hostage to national/international grain markets.

D. Regional Economies of the South

Slave plantations prospered in the Black Belt because of the high price of cotton on the world market. Many slaves previously involved in non-agricultural labor were reduced to cotton hands as planters concentrated their efforts on "king cotton."

Immediately before the Civil War, the South showed increased concentration of wealth in both land and slaves. About half of southern whites were yeoman farmers with an average of only 50 acres, mainly producing for their own consumption.

Although slavery discouraged immigrants from moving to the rural South, southern port cities showed relative ethnic diversity. For example, in Mobile, Alabama in 1860, 54 percent of skilled workers and 64 percent of unskilled labor were immigrants.

Slaves fought back against their owners by stealing and secretly selling the stolen goods to poor whites. Highly skilled slaves were often allowed to hire themselves out and keep part of their wages. Also, there were an increasing number of free blacks in the South, so the situation was not as clear cut as the concepts of white/free and black/slave.

E. A Free Labor Ideology in the North

The popular northern idea of "Free Labor" that held that workers should reap what they sowed was undercut by economic reality. Many New England farmers were forced off the land, while hand workers were hit hard by such industrial developments as the mechanization of the shoe industry. In seaport cities, wage earning, rather than being self-employed, became the norm.

Poor Irish Catholics sought to distance themselves from African Americans by claiming their white skin as a badge of privilege in comparison with former slaves. Women worked hard, but in the home, where they were not paid. White workers began to condemn their oppression in a system of wage slavery.

II. Individualism Versus Group Identity

Economic growth and new technology helped spawn group identities that labeled some people as inferior due to their nationality, language, religion, legal status, or skin color. While Plains Indians resisted these developments, African Americans and women fought for more rights within the emerging system.

A. Putting into Practice Ideas of Social Inferiority

Custom and economic competition led to ideas of gender and "racial" inferiority that then became codified in law. Social status in the United States can be seen in patterns of work. Anglos stereotyped all Chinese, Mexicans, and African Americans as promiscuous, crafty, and intellectually inferior to whites.

B. "A Teeming Nation" —America in Literature

Ideologies of ethnic/racial difference coexisted with the idea of American individualism, which stressed universal equality.

Some literature, like that written by Emerson, began to critique American materialism. Thoreau's *Walden* (1854) was eco-centric, while Walt Whitman's *Leaves of Grass* (1855) captured the nation's restlessness.

C. Challenges to Individualism

New American egotism had little meaning for Native Americans, who continued to celebrate the primacy of kinship and village over that of the individual.

African Americans in the North knew their fate was linked with southern slaves, since whites continued to lump all people of African descent together as "black."

Some women took to a collective identity of womanhood, although this took many varied forms. At the Seneca Falls Convention (1848), women linked their plight with that of slaves since both were exploited.

There was no single American identity in the middle of the nineteenth century.

III. The Paradox of Southern Political Power

In the early 1850s, the pro-slavery forces controlled all the branches of the federal government but increasingly felt insecure as the United States expanded westward.

A. Party System in Disarray

In 1848, the Free Soil Party attacked the idea that Whigs and Democrats could smooth over the question of slavery in the new territories. The new party stood for a no-slavery-in-the-new-lands policy. The Free Soil Party also supported aid for internal improvements, free land for settlers, and tariff protection for northern manufacturers.

By 1849, the South saw power slipping out of its hands and shifting toward an increasingly slavery-hostile North. Meanwhile, Abolitionists and blacks were helping slaves escape through a series of safe stops on the way north. This route became known as the Underground Railroad.

B. The Compromise of 1850

Crisis over the admission of non-slave California to the Union resulted in a compromise fashioned by Henry Clay and Daniel Webster with the rigidly pro-slavery John C. Calhoun.

California was admitted as a free state while New Mexico and Utah would later hold referendums to determine if they would allow slavery. In return, the South got a new harsher fugitive slave law, which required local and federal lawmen to return runaway slaves no matter where in the country they had escaped to.

Although the election of 1852 was relatively lackluster, it marked the beginning of a split in the national political parties.

C. Expansionism and Political Upheaval

Southern planters looked beyond the U.S. border in their quest to expand the slave system. Cuba, a Spanish colony, was a particular target and two "filibustering expeditions" made unsuccessful assaults on the island.

In 1855, pro-slavery mercenaries led by William Walker seized control of Nicaragua. Walker promoted slavery and was recognized by the U.S. government in 1856, although he was driven from power a year and a half later.

In 1853, Commodore Perry sailed a U.S. Naval fleet into Tokyo harbor and forced Japan to open up relations with the West.

The Kansas-Nebraska Act (1854) allowed the two territories to determine whether or not slavery would be allowed. This law also took away half of all the land that had been granted to the Plains Indians by treaty. Fearful that slavery would roll westward, northern Free Soilers were enraged.

The American Party, or "Know-Nothings" (1852), was established as a backlash against the increasing political power of immigrants, especially Irish Catholics.

D. The Republican Alliance

The Republican Party was established in 1854 by disaffected Whigs on the core belief that there should be no slavery in the new territories. The Republicans were an alliance of some northern Democrats and various antislavery elements. Many Republicans were racist and opposed black migration to the North, since their opposition to slavery was economic rather than moral.

In the 1856 presidential election, Republican John C. Fremont won 11 of the 16 northern states despite his defeat by Democrat James Buchanan.

Slavery had to expand to survive, as intensive cultivation was exhausting the soil of southern cotton fields while the planter elite needed new slave states admitted to the Union to preserve their power in Washington.

IV. The Deepening Conflict Over Slavery

Although adult white males were only a minority of the population, they were directly involved in establishing new political parties and in the congressional debates over slavery. In the 1850s, more and more ordinary people were drawn into the battle over slavery that was drawing America towards armed conflict.

A. The Rising Tide of Violence

The Fugitive Slave Law caused fear and alarm among many northerners as some African Americans fled to Canada. African Americans often staged dramatic rescues like that of Shadrach Minkins, who was freed from a courtroom and spirited to Montreal.

Women were not welcome in the various African American conventions called in response to slave owners' ever-increasing attempts to capture runaways. At the same time, black and white women became prominent supporters of abolitionism.

Publication of antislavery literature like *Uncle Tom's Cabin* (1852) began to spread the abolitionist argument to wide sections of the population, as did Frederick Law Olmsted's reports in the *New York Times*.

The territory of Kansas became engulfed in a regional Civil War as pro-slavery settlers fought Free Soilers and terrorism was employed on both sides.

Pro-slavery forces drew up the Lecompton Constitution that stated that even if voters rejected slavery, slaves already in the state would remain slaves. When President Buchanan supported this action, the Democratic Party began to split into Northern and Southern factions.

In 1856, when Senator Charles Sumner condemned the pro-slavery crimes against Kansas, a South Carolina congressman beat him into unconsciousness.

B. The Dred Scott Decision

In 1857, Dred Scott, a former slave, sued in federal court, maintaining that he had become free once his master had taken him into a free state. The Supreme Court ruled that even in free states, slaves remained slaves. This decision destroyed previous compromises and threatened free people of color while potentially expanding slavery to the North.

Even those Northerners who were not abolitionists feared that jobs and farms might be lost to an expanding slave plantation system.

C. The Lincoln-Douglas Debates

As political conflict increased, the 1858 congressional elections were seen as especially important. The most notable contest was between Democrat Stephen R. Douglas and Republican Abraham Lincoln for a Senate seat from the state of Illinois. Although Lincoln lost, his campaign established him as one of the best-known leaders of the new Republican Party.

D. Harpers Ferry and the Presidential Election of 1860

Abolitionist John Brown and nineteen others attacked a federal arsenal in Harpers Ferry, Virginia in October 1859. Brown planned to take the weapons he captured there and distribute them to slaves, thereby causing a general slave rebellion. Captured by Marines under the command of Robert E. Lee, Brown was condemned and hanged, but before he died, he predicted "that the crimes of this guilty land will never be purged away, but with blood."

In 1860, the Democratic Party split, with Northerners nominating Stephen Douglas while Southern Democrats nominated John C. Breckinridge. Meanwhile, a group who still thought compromise was possible formed the Constitutional Union Party and selected John Bell to run for president.

Republicans meeting in Chicago chose moderate Abe Lincoln, who promised something for all white men, even recent European immigrants, but held out no promises for Spanish speakers, Chinese, free blacks, Indians, or women.

In the 1850s, more Northerners came to fear the slave system as an attack on their way of life even if they held little sympathy for the African American slaves themselves. In the same manner, in the South, whites, including both planters and the poor, united behind an ill-defined sense of white skin privilege known as the "southern way of life."

Identification

Explain the significance of each of the following:

1.   Treaty of Guadalupe Hidalgo (1848):

2.   Fugitive Slave Law:

3.   "Coolies":

4.   "Great American Desert":

5.   Gadsden Purchase:

6.   Tejanos:

7.   Texas Rangers:

8.   "Cortina's War":

9.   John Deere's steel plow:

10.   Black Belt:

11.   "Free Labor":

12.   Frederick Douglass:

13.   "Wage slavery":

14.   *Walden* (1854):

15.   *Leaves of Grass* (1855):

16. Seneca Falls Convention (1848):

17. Free Soil Party:

18. Harriet Tubman:

19. Underground Railroad:

20. John C. Calhoun:

21. William Walker:

22. "Manifest Destiny":

23. Kansas-Nebraska Act (1854):

24. Know-Nothings:

25. *Uncle Tom's Cabin* (1852):

26. John Brown:

27. Lecompton Constitution:

28. Dred Scott v. Sanford (1857):

29. Constitutional Union Party:

30. "southern way of life":

Multiple Choice Questions:

1. Which of the following is NOT a result of the Mexican War?
   A. The United States gained over one-half million square miles of territory.
   B. Thousands of Mexicans and Indians found themselves in U.S. territory.
   C. The territories of Arizona and New Mexico quickly became states.
   D. Free passage to and from the U.S. was guaranteed.
   E. By treaty, Mexicans living in the new territories were guaranteed U.S. citizenship rights.
   Page References: 395–396

2. By the 1850s, the Cherokee had
   A. given up on the idea of education as a means of advancement.
   B. created a flourishing print culture in their own language.
   C. mostly moved westward to southern Utah.
   D. rejected the culture of European Americans.
   E. re-embraced Native American paganism.
   Page Reference: 397

3. The free labor ideology of the 1850s
   A. supported slavery as the ultimate form of free labor.
   B. was mainly supported by the white people of the South.
   C. became extremely popular among Irish Catholics.
   D. held that workers should reap what they sow.
   E. promoted the right of women to the vote and equal rights.
   Page Reference: 401

4. In the mid-nineteenth century, California officials justified the inferiority of African Americans, Hispanics, and immigrants by saying
   A. those people had not entered the United States legally.
   B. non-Christians had no legal rights in the U.S.
   C. these groups were not of white blood.
   D. minorities failed to get the proper education necessary to prosper.
   E. only those with type AB blood should have full rights.
   Page Reference: 403

5. The author of the famous book *Leaves of Grass* written in 1855 was
   A. Walt Whitman.
   B. Henry David Thoreau.
   C. Frederick Douglass.
   D. John Greenleaf Whitter.
   E. Catherine Beecher.
   Page Reference: 405

6. The slave owners in the South were worried about abolitionism in the 1850s despite
   A. the fact that most slaves were happy.
   B. dominating the federal government.
   C. hiring Indians to replace African Americans.
   D. worldwide moral support for the southern way of life.
   E. the growth of the underground railroad.
   Page Reference: 408

7. The underground railroad consisted of
   A. the nation's first subway system in Philadelphia.
   B. secret subsidies given by large farmers to rail corporations.
   C. the practice of running train tracks below sea level.
   D. a wild plan by a Texas inventor that never worked.
   E. a network of safe stops whereby slaves were smuggled to freedom in the North or Canada.
   Page Reference: 410

8. In 1855, pro-slavery adventurer, Tennessee-born William Walker seized control of Nicaragua and
   A. abolished slavery in that nation.
   B. won U.S. recognition for his regime the following year.
   C. made it profitable because of Mexican migrant labor.
   D. was then elected by a grateful Nicaraguan public to the presidency.
   E. attempted to pull it out of the Union.
   Page Reference: 412

9. In March 1854, the Republican Party was formed based on the core idea that
   A. the Whigs had to be defeated at all costs.
   B. the Democratic Party could and should be reformed.
   C. President Buchanan must be impeached.
   D. the North must move away from the use of slave labor.
   E. slavery must not be allowed to spread into the western territories.
   Page Reference: 413

10. In the Presidential election of 1856, Millard Fillmore ran as the candidate of what party?
    A. American
    B. Republican
    C. Free Soil
    D. Democratic
    E. Federalist
    Page Reference: 414

11. After the Fugitive Slave Act of 1850 led to the pursuit of former slaves into the North,
    A. African Americans began marrying white people.
    B. abolitionists gave up their cause as hopeless.
    C. abolitionists often used force to free captives or resist re-enslavement.
    D. European Americans refused to go to church.
    E. the slave owners of the South had no more problems.
    Page Reference: 415

12. By 1855, the territory of Kansas was
    A. overwhelmingly in favor of the slave system.
    B. becoming engulfed in a regional civil war.
    C. given a state constitution that outlawed slavery completely.
    D. spared the violence that shook nearby Missouri.
    E. preparing to impeach Senator Charles Sumner.
    Page Reference: 417

13. John Brown led a raid on Harpers Ferry in the hopes of
    A. becoming a hero to southern whites.
    B. preventing cheap Chinese-imported products.
    C. forcing an invasion of Cuba.
    D. freeing the slaves.
    E. having his revenge on U.S. Grant.
    Page Reference: 420

14. In 1860, Abraham Lincoln was elected President
    A. with only about 40 percent of the popular vote.
    B. as the candidate of the Constitutional Union party.
    C. largely because of the support of African American voters.
    D. because he was able to carry about half of the southern states.
    E. in a landslide, winning almost two-thirds of the vote.
    Page Reference: 421

15. The northern working class feared the expansion of slavery into the territories even if they
    A. knew it would be good for America.
    B. knew slaves lowered the cost of living.
    C. did not care about their economic opportunities.
    D. voted for pro-slavery candidates in 1860.
    E. cared little about the rights of slaves.
    Page Reference: 421

MAP QUESTION

After looking at Map 13.2, analyze the impact of the Underground Railroad on the slave system.

ENVISIONING HISTORY

Explain the different ways that U.S. elections have changed from when this painting was completed until the present. What do you think is the most important change?

THE WIDER WORLD

Analyze how and why slavery was abolished in different places at different times? How does the United States compare with other nations?

INTERPRETING HISTORY

Discuss what you agree and disagree with in the essay by Professor Howe. What do you think explains his views?

CONNECTING HISTORY

Detail various forms of unfree labor, while explaining how each restricts the freedom of the individual in very specific ways. What do you think accounts for the continued existence of unfree labor in the contemporary world? How, if at all, is this different than the past?

Answers to Multiple Choice Questions:

1.	C	15.	E
2.	B		
3.	D		
4.	C		
5.	A		
6.	B		
7.	E		
8.	B		
9.	E		
10.	A		
11.	C		
12.	B		
13.	D		
14.	A		

Chapter 14
Fight to Gain a Country: The Civil War

Learning Objectives:

After reading Chapter 14, you should be able to:

1. Detail the reasons behind the secession impulse.
2. Explain the preparations the South undertook to fight the North.
3. Understand what factors inhibited the South from successfully mobilizing for war.
4. Discuss the problems the Confederacy had in enlisting the support of Indians and immigrants.
5. Analyze the contradictions in the early Republican war policy.
6. Detail the ravages of war in the summer of 1862.
7. Explain the reasons behind and the effect of the Emancipation Proclamation.
8. Discuss the continuing obstacles to the Confederacy's overall strategy.
9. Understand how African Americans struggled for liberation during the Civil War.
10. Comprehend the significance of the continuing fight against prejudice in North and South.
11. Understand how disaffection grew within the Confederacy as the war went on.
12. Discuss what caused the tide of war to turn against the South.
13. Analyze the reasons for civil unrest in the North.
14. Detail the desperation of the South by 1863.
15. Understand the nature of the "hard war" towards African Americans and Indians.
16. Discuss the last days of the Confederacy.

Time Line

1860
Abraham Lincoln elected president
South Carolina seceded from the Union

1861
Abraham Lincoln sworn in as president
Attack on Fort Sumter
Battle of Bull Run
Lincoln gave General Scott power to suspend writ of habeas corpus

1862
Democrats picked up strength in Congressional elections

1863
Emancipation Proclamation freed slaves in rebel territory
North abandoned policy of conciliation towards South
Battle of Gettysburg
General U.S. Grant captured Vicksburg
Antiblack draft riots in New York City by mainly Irish mobs

1864
Lincoln reelected over Democratic candidate George McClellan
General Sherman's march to the sea took Atlanta and then Savannah

1865
Confederate General Lee surrendered to Grant, Civil War ends
Lincoln assassinated by John Wilkes Booth, a Confederate supporter

I. Mobilization for War, 1861-1862

A. The Secession Impulse

Although political support for newly elected President Lincoln seemed slim and his party controlled neither Congress nor the Supreme Court, the southern elite felt threatened by the new president's promise to halt the expansion of slavery into the western territories. Slave owners thought it was only a matter of time before the North encouraged any number of attacks on the southern way of life. Two last ditch attempts at compromise failed and Lincoln's pleas for national unity fell on deaf ears. When Lincoln continued to supply Fort Sumter, a union fort in South Carolina, Confederates began firing on the federal facility and forced its surrender in thirty-three hours. In response, Lincoln called for 75,000 volunteers to put down the rebellion and ordered a blockade of southern ports. These actions pushed the hesitating states of the upper South to join the Confederacy.

The manner in which the southern states left the union would reveal the political differences that would plague the Confederacy. Most states left after conventions dominated by slave owners with little regard for the desire of poor Southerners for compromise. The Border States of Missouri, Kentucky, Maryland, and Delaware remained in the Union despite sizable pro-Confederate sentiment.

B. Preparing to Fight

Both sides faced problems as they prepared to fight. North and South alike had to find large numbers of men to fight and produce massive amounts of cannon, ammunition, and food. With huge stockpiles of cotton and food, Southerners were confident they could force the North into accepting secession by fighting a defensive war that would bleed Union armies that advanced into Confederate territory. The North, without much of a strategy, counted on its superior numbers. It controlled 90 percent of manufacturing and three-quarters of the railroads, while its population of 22 million was far larger than the South's 9 million. Both sides appealed to their common Revolutionary heritage, with the South stressing unfair taxation and states' rights as the North put forth the glories of the Union.

C. Barriers to Southern Mobilization

While the South won the first battle of 1861 at Bull Run, Southerners only gradually realized that they needed to industrialize their economy and centralize their government if they were to ultimately win. As the northern blockade of southern ports disrupted established trade, the Confederacy found itself without money from customs duties and was forced to raise taxes and sell bonds. The Confederate Treasury also responded by printing money at such a fast rate that the real value of Confederate dollars declined steadily until they were worth only 1.6 cents near the war's end.

Raising an army and forcing slaves to work for the military met strong resistance from many parts of southern society. Yeoman farmers resented the draft of their sons while slave owners resisted parting with their slaves even in a fight to save slavery. When the Confederate call for volunteers failed to produce enough men, Jefferson Davis, President of the Confederacy, received the power to conscript men between the ages of eighteen and thirty-five for up to three years. Wealthy men could avoid the draft by paying $300 for a substitute. This was the first draft in the history of North America.

D. Indians in the Service of the Confederacy

The South was unable to fully mobilize Native Americans as only gradually and reluctantly did most southern tribes agree to join the fight. Those who fought often frustrated their Confederate commanders by their desire to continue with traditional battle tactics rather than line up in long straight lines. Many Native Americans, resentful of broken promises made by the Confederacy, joined up with the Union forces.

E. The Ethnic Confederacy

The Confederacy claimed that their army was composed of native-born soldiers while the Union ranks were filled with the Irish, Dutch, Scotch, and, most of all, Germans. This is misleading, as immigrants were actually under-represented in the northern army while the South was more multicultural than many white Southerners realized. Immigrant workers from southern cities filled the ranks of the Confederate army and a Jewish slaveholder served in the cabinet.

On the other hand, many immigrants in the South remained suspect, particularly Germans in Texas. Although 2,500 men of Spanish descent joined the Confederate army, many claimed they were Mexican citizens and therefore not required to participate.

II. The Course of the War, 1862-1864

A. The Republicans' War

On April 27, 1861, Lincoln gave General Winfield Scott the power to suspend the writ of habeas corpus in Baltimore. By the end of the year, this measure, which was designed to target southern sympathizers, was applied to most of the North. Democrats denounced the president as a tyrant, yet abolitionists were frustrated with Lincoln's conciliatory policy toward the South and Union slaveholders. Wartime business was a blessing for enterprising Northerners like McCormick and Rockefeller who made fortunes as war profiteers. The South likewise had speculators who enriched themselves by selling goods at extremely high prices.

Republicans centralized wartime operation and in 1861 created the U.S. Sanitary Commission, which recruited medical personnel. During the war, as many as 20,000 white and black women served as nurses, cooks, and laundresses in northern military hospitals. Republicans used their control of the federal government to promote economic development and education by establishing homesteads, subsidizing railroads, and creating a system of land-grant colleges. For the first eighteen months, the northern military strategy reflected an indifference to the rights or welfare of African Americans. Slaves who ran to Union lines would be returned to their masters if the slave owner was a Unionist.

B. The Ravages of War

While the Confederacy was successful on the battlefield in 1862, it suffered from some 20,000 slaves fleeing to the North and helping the Union with information and manual labor. The North suffered from the incompetence of General George McClellan and an overly forgiving attitude towards the South. The summer of 1862 showed the problems both sides faced in fighting the war during warm weather, when disease killed twice as many soldiers as bullets. In the West, the Union army conducted savage campaigns against Indian tribes. In the East, the Union won a victory at Antietam at the cost of 20,000 lives. Women increasingly served as nurses in the South, tending the wounded despite prejudice that this was work too horrible for a woman.

C. The Emancipation Proclamation

On January 1, 1863, Lincoln issued the Emancipation Proclamation, which freed slaves in Confederate territory. By this act, Lincoln hoped to infuse the war with a moral purpose while, at the same time, encouraging southern blacks to join the U.S. Army. Ironically, nearly one million African American slaves were excluded from this act since they lived in loyal Border States. The Emancipation Proclamation excited abolitionists but the growing death toll and higher taxes caused dissent to grow.

D. Persistent Obstacles to the Confederacy's Grand Strategy

By the end of 1861, the North had established beachheads in Confederate territory all along the East Coast. The Confederacy pinned great hopes on gaining the support of, or at least the recognition from, European powers, particularly England. They were unsuccessful, as the South's cotton proved not to be indispensable and English workers fought fiercely and successfully against recognition of the South. The Confederacy also failed to win the support of Mexican President Benito Juarez, who kept Mexico a friend of the Union. All hope for diplomatic recognition of the South faded with Union victories at Antietam and Perryville, combined with the powerful effect of the soon-to-be announced Emancipation Proclamation.

III. The Other War: African American Struggles for Liberation

A. The Unfolding of Freedom

African Americans fought in ways that whites could neither understand nor expect. Georgia slave Nancy Johnson and her family are a noteworthy example. Nancy and her husband Boston harbored an escaped Union prisoner of war and later marveled at having a white man sit in their house. By the end of the war, Nancy and Boston Johnson had sheltered and fed others they saw as allies, from deserters from the Confederate army to poor whites opposed to the war and without any slaves.

As the war approached the end, Johnson told her mistress she would no longer work without wages. Instead of being able to order Nancy to work, the slave owner was reduced to cajoling, intimidating, and making promises in order to get her to labor. Still, Johnson's experience with the Union army was not positive. In January 1865, Union troops raided the plantation and stole most of the family's possessions in an orgy of looting. Neither Nancy nor Boston could believe that Yankees could be so mean.

B. Enemies Within the Confederacy

Slaveholding whites were shocked to discover that they could not always count on the loyalty of their slaves. Soon after the war began, many white slave owners wondered if their slaves would one day kill them in their beds. African American slaves waited for a chance to steal away at night or even in broad daylight, as slaves fled their plantations to seek safety and paid labor behind Union lines. In July 1862, the Union's Second Confiscation Act held that slaves of Confederates would be considered captives of war and shall be forever free.

C. The Ongoing Fight Against Prejudice

The Emancipation Proclamation inspired black men in the North to join the Union armed forces. Although until late in the war they were paid less than whites and denied advancement, African American soldiers wore their uniforms proudly as they were fighting for freedom. Typically, blacks were barred from taking up arms and relegated to dangerous fatigue work. As a result, for every black soldier killed in action, ten died of disease. Southern blacks welcomed the northern army but often suffered from harsh treatment by their liberators, who considered them less than equal.

IV. Battle Fronts and Home Fronts in 1863

A. Disaffection in the Confederacy

The war deeply affected Southerners, who saw their land destroyed by fighting and their lives disrupted by war preparations. Throughout the South were communities resentful of what ordinary whites saw as the Richmond elite, that is, the leaders of the Confederacy. As many as one-third of all Confederate soldiers were absent without leave at any time during the war. Poor women resisted the orders of the Jefferson Davis administration while resentful of the extravagant wartime lifestyle of the southern elite. In April 1863, hundreds of Richmond women ransacked stores in search of food and were only dispersed when President Davis threatened to have the army shoot them. Other white women leaped to give their aid to the Confederacy in a variety of roles, ranging from spies to textile factory workers.

B. The Tide Turns Against the South

In December 1862, Union General Burnside blundered into a major defeat at Fredericksburg, Virginia. Burnside was replaced by General "Fighting Joe" Hooker, who fought Confederate Generals Lee and Stonewall Jackson at Chancellorsville, Virginia. Although Hooker lost, the battle claimed the life of the Confederate General Jackson, an important loss for the South. Hoping to follow up his victory, Robert E. Lee led Confederate troops into Pennsylvania, a move he thought would encourage northern Peace Democrats and impress foreign powers. In a three-day battle at Gettysburg in July 1863, 23,000 Union and 28,000 Confederate troops were killed. Lee saw one-third of his men killed or wounded. The following day, Ulysses S. Grant captured Vicksburg for the Union.

C. Civil Unrest in the North

Not all of the North joined in the celebration over the victory at Gettysburg. Even strong Union supporters were tired of high taxes, inflated prices, and the ever-growing death toll. Following a military draft begun on July 1, northern white workers, particularly the Irish, rose up both in angry protest over the wealthy being able to buy substitutes and in not wishing to fight for their black workplace competition. Laborers in New York City, Hartford, Troy, Newark, and Boston went on a rampage and 105 people died before the antiblack riots were suppressed by federal troops. To prevent further outbreaks, 20,000 Union soldiers were stationed in New York so that on August 19, the draft could continue.

D. The Desperate South

The South had to deal not only with dissent at home but also with the terrible losses suffered at Gettysburg and Vicksburg. Confederate President Jefferson Davis urged his supporters to call upon God for mercy. Although Confederate military leaders shunned guerilla warfare, William Clarke Quantrill attacked Lawrence, Kansas and 450 Southerners under his command killed 150 civilians. The Quantrill raid showed how desperate some Confederates had become. The victories of Grant and the Union at Missionary Ridge and Lookout Mountain in Tennessee caused both France and England to draw back from selling the Confederacy warships or giving diplomatic recognition.

V. The Prolonged Defeat of the Confederacy, 1864-1865

A. "Hard War" Toward African Americans and Native Americans

"Hard war" is not the same as "total war," where the entire civilian population is a target. Yet, Confederate actions toward black soldiers and Union policies toward Native American rebels showed elements of total war. Black soldiers who surrendered to Confederate forces were systematically murdered, while wounded African American troops were bayoneted or burned alive. Meanwhile, northern forces in the west attacked Native Americans without any regard for the conventions of warfare. Union Col. John M. Chivington made it a policy to kill all Native Americans, even children.

B. "Father Abraham"

Lincoln was indifferent to the plight of Native Americans but made a noble defense of democracy among white men. His reelection in 1864 was made easier by a string of Union military victories and the Democratic peace program, which alienated northern troops who gave Lincoln three-quarters of their votes. Although Lincoln had little military experience, he had a superior grasp of strategy and was popular with the average northern soldier.

C. Sherman's March from Atlanta to the Sea

The South's physical environment had shaped the course of the Civil War. In turn, the war changed the environment, as demonstrated by Sherman's March to the Sea. After taking Atlanta in the summer of 1864, Union General William Tecumseh Sherman marched an army of 60,000 infantry and 5,500 cavalry to the coast. Utilizing runaway slaves to assist his engineers, Sherman was able to clear the obstacles left behind by retreating Confederates. He also destroyed all the railroads he came upon while forgoing long supply trains and having his men live off the land. With the capture of Savannah, the southern cause was all but lost.

D. The Last Days of the Confederacy

The Confederacy, which had begun the war as a loose collection of rural states, was now a centralized war machine. It was, however, a war machine running out of men. The South was so desperate that it considered freeing the slaves in order to turn them into Confederate soldiers. Meanwhile, the Union went from victory to victory as Sherman seized Atlanta in 1864 on his march to the sea. Along the way, Sherman liberated Andersonville, the infamous Confederate POW camp where 13,000 Union prisoners had died of starvation and neglect. The commander of Andersonville was to be the only Confederate officer to be executed for war crimes.

By April, 1865, the war was all but over, with Grant seizing the Confederate capital of Richmond on April 3. Finally, General Lee surrendered what remained of his army on April 9. The amazingly generous surrender terms, which allowed the rebels to keep their horses and promised no trials for treason, showed a mutual respect that would later allow northern and southern whites to unite against people of color. Lincoln was not to play a part in the future of the nation, as he was murdered by John Wilkes Booth, a Confederate supporter who feared the president would give blacks citizenship.

Identification

Explain the significance of each of the following:

1.   Stephen A. Douglas:

2.   Fort Sumter:

3.   Jefferson Davis:

4.   Suspension of writ of habeas corpus (1861):

5.   U.S. Sanitary Commission:

6.   Ulysses S. Grant:

7.   Land-grant colleges:

8.   Stonewall Jackson:

9.   Emancipation Proclamation:

10.   *Trent* affair:

11.   Second Confiscation Act (1862):

12.   54th Massachusetts regiment:

13.   General George McClellan:

14.   Copperhead:

15. Vicksburg:

16. 1863 Riots in New York City:

17. William Clarke Quantrill:

18. Fort Pillow:

19. Col. John M. Chivington:

20. Admiral David G. Farragut:

21. Andersonville Prison:

22. Sherman's March to the sea (1864-1865):

23. General Robert E. Lee:

24. Henry Wirz:

25. "Father Abraham":

Multiple Choice Questions:

1. Abraham Lincoln was elected president in 1860 although
  A. he lost in the electoral college.
  B. 60 percent of voters supported other candidates.
  C. Congress passed into the hands of the Republicans.
  D. he only carried states in the South.
  E. less than a fourth northern voters supported him.
  Page Reference: 425

2.	The southern states began to leave the Union because
A. they welcomed the new Republican president.
B. lower tariffs were destroying their state finances.
C. the North had a clear majority on the Supreme Court.
D. Lincoln threatened to enslave white Southerners.
E. they feared that the balance of power had changed decisively in favor of the North.
Page Reference: 426

3.	The Southerners who tended to withhold their support from the Confederacy were
A. enslaved black workers.
B. slave owners.
C. plantation owners who grew cotton.
D. white racists who believed in African American inferiority.
E. southern-born graduates of West Point.
Page Reference: 427

4.	The newly formed Confederacy had the advantage of
A. a larger population.
B. more naval warships and experienced sailors.
C. more experienced military leaders and trained soldiers.
D. more developed industry.
E. knowing that all their slaves were loyal to their masters.
Page Reference: 428

5.	During the Civil War, the North had the advantage of having
A. 90 percent of manufacturing capacity.
B. a diversified economy that produced grain as well as textiles.
C. control of the federal government and its bureaucratic infrastructure.
D. a much larger population.
E. All of the above.
Page Reference: 428

6.	To finance the Confederate government, the South turned to
A	lower taxes to stimulate the economy.
B. printing money at a furious rate.
C. the always large sums raised by custom duties.
D. the generous contributions of German immigrants.
E. secret support from northern abolitionists.
Page Reference: 432

7.	Short of volunteers, the Confederacy in March 1862
A. began to allow free blacks to serve in the Confederate armed forces.
B. began to draft women.
C. started to accept immigrants into their military.
D. established the first military conscription on the North American continent.
E. began buying slaves to fight in the Confederate army.
Page Reference: 433

8. In April, 1861, Lincoln gave General Winfield Scott the power to
   A. buy supplies for the Union army.
   B. return fire if attacked by Confederate troops.
   C. suspend the writ of habeas corpus in Baltimore.
   D. award medals for bravery under fire.
   E. organize an invasion force destined for Florida.
   Page Reference: 436

9. President Lincoln, in September, 1861, revoked an order by General Fremont
   A. that would have freed slaves owned by Confederates in Missouri.
   B. ordering the use of rapid fire cannons.
   C. ending charges into cannon fire.
   D. demanding an end to his troops being given bad food.
   E. declaring Missouri a part of the Confederacy.
   Page Reference: 437

10. The Emancipation Proclamation would, it was hoped,
   A. cause southern blacks to join the Union army.
   B. cause Copperheads to become more supportive of Lincoln.
   C. cause an end to slavery in the Border States.
   D. rally southern slave owners to the Union cause.
   E. All of the above.
   Page Reference: 441

11. The Confederacy approached Mexico for support and found that
   A. Mexico was willing to do whatever it could to help break up the United States.
   B. the President of Mexico assumed the South would win and was ready to help.
   C. the Emancipation Proclamation had angered the Mexican people.
   D. Benito Juarez remained an ally of the United States.
   E. they were too busy fighting France to help out.
   Page Reference: 442

12. Some southern whites undermined the Confederacy as witness that
   A. they used African Americans as soldiers.
   B. one-third of Confederate soldiers were absent without leave at any one time.
   C. they treated captured Black soldiers as well as they did white Northerners.
   D. they stole from those captured.
   E. None of the above
   Page Reference: 446

13. Among the reasons for disaffection in the Confederacy was
    A. a 10 percent tax-in-kind on produce.
    B. food shortages.
    C. resentment at the extravagant wartime lifestyle of the wealthy.
    D. support for the North among some poor whites.
    E. All of the above.
    Page Reference: 446

14. During the Presidential Election of 1864, Abraham Lincoln
    A. lost the popular vote to George McClellan.
    B. survived a series of Union defeats during the election campaign.
    C. won three-quarters of the army's vote.
    D. expressed shock that General Sherman burned Atlanta.
    E. ran with General Sherman as his Vice-Presidential candidate.
    Page Reference: 452

15. Sherman's March to the Sea became
    A. famous for its foraging off the countryside.
    B. repudiated by Lincoln because it was too harsh on the South.
    C. a propaganda victory although a military defeat.
    D. very careful not to harm southern industrial infrastructure like railroads.
    E. unable to take Atlanta because of General Robert E. Lee's timely arrival.
    Page Reference: 454

MAP QUESTION:

After looking at Map 14.5, discuss the contribution of African American soldiers in the Union cause. How would the war have been different if blacks had not become soldiers for the North? What if the South had abolished slavery and armed its black residents?

ENVISIONING HISTORY

After carefully examining the photo of the Civil War encampment, discuss what this shows about the nature of warfare at the time of the American Civil War.

THE WIDER WORLD

What factors led to the Civil War being so much bloodier than almost all the other wars the U.S. has fought? Explain!

CONNECTING HISTORY

Discuss the history of civil disorder in wartime. Why are protests violent at some times but peaceful at others? Give examples.

INTERPRETING HISTORY

What were the motivations that caused John B. Spiece to object to the impressment of slaves? Do you think his arguments reveal the contradictions of the southern slave system? Why or why not?

Answers to Multiple Choice Questions

1. B
2. E
3. A
4. C
5. E
6. B
7. D
8. C
9. A
10. A
11. D
12. B
13. E
14. C
15. A

Chapter 15
In the Wake of War: Consolidating a Triumphant Union, 1865–1877

Learning Objectives:

After reading Chapter 15, you should be able to:

1. Understand how the Civil War set the stage for postwar policies.
2. Explain the significant aspects of presidential Reconstruction policies, 1865-1867.
3. Discuss the southern postwar labor problem and how it affected freed slaves and poor whites.
4. Contrast Congressional or Radical Reconstruction with policies of President Johnson.
5. Detail the situation of isolated Indian territories in the West.
6. Explain the interaction of labor and land in the West.
7. Discuss the origins of the Woman Suffrage Movement.
8. Understand the significance of political corruption and the decline in Republican idealism.

Time Line

1865
Civil War ended
Freedmen's Bureau established
Thirteenth Amendment approved

1866
National Labor Union (NLU) established
Equal Rights Association formed to link rights of women with African Americans
President Andrew Johnson vetoed Civil Rights Bill and expansion of Freedmen's Bureau

1867
Alaska purchased from Russia

1868
Ulysses S. Grant elected president

1871
Ku Klux Klan Act punished conspiracies to deny rights to citizens

1872
U. S. Grant reelected president over Democrat Horace Greeley

1873
Nationwide depression hit U.S.

1876
General George Custer defeated at Little Big Horn in Montana
Republican Hayes became president after deal with Southern Democrats

1877
Compromise between northern Republicans and Southern Democrats ended Reconstruction

Chapter Overview

In March 1865, the federal government agreed to help set up schools for blacks under the auspices of the newly created Freedmen's Bureau.

Republican congressmen wanted to reconstruct the South by having African Americans own land and become full citizens. Freedmen sought to free themselves from white control while establishing control over their work, families, and churches. President Andrew Johnson wished to restore prewar power relations that placed blacks in the position of being dependent labor.

The Republican Party stood for strong national government while the Democrats argued for states' rights.

The U.S. Army attacked the Plains Indians when some Native Americans refused to abandon their nomadic way of life.

Between 1862 and 1872, the federal government gave the railroads millions of dollars in cash and a hundred million acres of public land. Meanwhile in the South, the scars of war were visible everywhere as economic growth unleashed after the conflict transformed the physical landscape of the country.

There was dissent from those who felt that Republicans would serve white men of property only. Women wanted the right to vote, while workers believed themselves at the mercy of employers and so formed a national labor union in 1866.

I. The Struggle Over the South

Republicans argued among themselves over how far government should go to protect the freedmen. President Johnson did not want blacks to become independent of white landowners.

Blacks sought socioeconomic self-determination and many traveled around looking for family members lost during slavery.

A. Wartime Preludes to Postwar Policies

In November 1861, northern forces captured the Sea Islands (off of the Carolinas). When the planters fled, ten thousand slaves stayed behind and began to fish and raise corn to feed their families. White teachers, missionaries, and investors came, as well. The blacks welcomed the first two groups but resisted the capitalists' attempts to get them to grow cotton. In southern Louisiana, the Union army forced blacks back to work on plantations (supposedly now for wages). The former slaves resisted and even some northern soldiers contested the policy. These two examples show Republican commitment to preserving the plantation economy as blacks fought to free themselves from white control.

Lincoln proposed a 10 percent plan whereby a state could form a new government if 10 percent of those who voted in 1860 pledged allegiance to the Union. In 1864, Congress passed the Wade-Davis bill, which would require a majority of voters to take a loyalty oath. Lincoln vetoed this law.

B. Presidential Reconstruction, 1865-1867

President Johnson pushed the 10 percent plan and wanted blacks to remain as dependent farm laborers. His policies caused resentment among congressional Republicans, who thought them too lenient.

Readmitted southern states passed "Black Codes," which sought to reduce the freedmen to neo-slavery by forcing them to work on the land while denying them the right to vote, to serve on juries, and a number of other civil rights. In January 1865, Congress approved the Thirteenth Amendment, which abolished slavery.

President Johnson vetoed two important bills: an extension of the Freedmen's Bureau and the Civil Rights Bill of 1866. Congress overrode both vetoes and in June 1866 passed the Fourteenth Amendment, which guaranteed former slaves citizenship rights, denied many former rebels the right to hold office, and voided the Confederate debt.

Many Northerners moved south to invest in land, while some former southern white Whigs allied with northern Republicans. Southern Democrats called these men "Scalawags."

In 1866, the Ku Klux Klan was formed and later grew into a white supremacist terrorist organization that used murder and violence to reassert white power.

In the November, 1866 Congressional elections, the Republicans won a two-thirds majority in both houses of Congress. They hoped that this would enable them to override President Johnson and his expected vetoes.

C. The Southern Postwar Labor Policies

This period saw a struggle over who should toil in the fields and under what conditions. Whites complained that black women stayed home with their children rather than work in the fields.

The Freedmen's Bureau served as a mediator between freed people and southern whites while encouraging a free labor system with annual labor contracts. Yet it was understaffed and under-funded. Blacks had to negotiate with white landowners, although the former slaves had little to offer but their own labor.

General Sherman issued Field Order #15, dividing the Sea Islands and the coastal region south of Charleston into forty-acre plots for freed families. He also lent mules to help with planting. A few months after the Civil War ended, the War Department gave in to white pressure and repealed the order.

The Freedmen's Bureau varied greatly in effectiveness. It helped blacks a good deal in some areas but had little impact elsewhere.

Within a few years after the war, the sharecropping system began to develop. Poor families would get supplies and the use of land. At harvest, they were to repay the landowner, but often the sharecroppers remained in debt.

D. Building Free Communities

Some black communities were divided by class, with formerly-free, skilled, and literate people assuming leadership over the illiterate field hands. Light-skinned free people of color, who often spoke French, were more likely to own property and have an education than English-speaking, dark-skinned freedpeople. Most black communities united around the demand for full citizenship rights enforced by the federal military.

Freedpeople in some areas allied with poor whites who had also suffered at the hands of the planter class. Networks of freedpeople created their own churches and schools.

Black families took care of elderly or poor relations and chose to have mothers stay home with their children.

Resentment against black advancement and pride caused many whites to form white supremacist organizations: Young Men's Democratic Clubs, White Brotherhood, Knights of the White Camelia, and, of course, the Ku Klux Klan.

E. Congressional Reconstruction: The Radicals' Plan

The Reconstruction Act of 1867 stripped thousands of former confederates of the right to vote. Former confederate states would not be readmitted until they ratified the Fourteenth Amendment and guaranteed black men the right to vote. The South was divided into five military districts. The Tenure of Office Act was passed by Republicans to protect Secretary of War Edwin Stanton from being dismissed by the president, while the Command of the Army Act required President Johnson to have approval from Ulysses S. Grant for all military orders.

Republicans threw their support behind an insurgent southern Republican party which they hoped could take over the South with the votes of freed black men and white Republicans. Southern Republican organizations, called Union Leagues, gave a political voice to many black leaders. About two thousand black men were elected to local office during Reconstruction, including sixteen congressmen, all of whom showed interest in being active, engaged citizens.

Newly reconstructed southern legislatures established public schools, fairer taxation, bargaining rights for plantation workers, and integrated public transportation and accommodations as well as public works like railroads. Although Southern Democrats and some historians have accused Reconstruction governments of being corrupt, they were as honest as those before or after their tenure.

In early 1868, President Johnson fired Secretary of War Stanton in violation of the Tenure of Office Act. Shortly afterward, Congress impeached Johnson. Johnson survived the removal motion by one vote but afterwards withdrew from policymaking.

In November 1868, U. S. Grant was elected president. By the end of 1868, Arkansas, North Carolina, South Carolina, Louisiana, Tennessee, Alabama, and Florida were readmitted to the Union, followed by Mississippi, Virginia, Georgia, and Texas two years later.

Democrats in the South soon resorted to wholesale election fraud and violence against freedpeople. In 1871, Congress passed the Ku Klux Klan Act, which punished conspiracies to deny rights to citizens. Despite this, many blacks continued to be terrorized.

F. Remarkable Career of Blanche K. Bruce

The career of Bruce reveals the possibilities and limitations for the rising black leadership during Reconstruction. Educated at Oberlin College, Bruce became a rich man and was elected to the U.S. Senate. When he lost his Senate seat in 1881, Bruce and his wife moved to Washington and he became a member of the city's African American elite. In the end, his success was to distance him from the average poor African American.

II. Claiming Territory for the Union

Joining the nation together both economically and politically was the Republican goal. To achieve this, both technology and military power would be utilized. Railroads became a vital part of national integration. In 1869, railroads from the East and West Coasts joined together in Utah. Meanwhile, the U.S. Cavalry attacked the Plains Indians. Between 1865 and 1890, the U.S. Army mounted a dozen different campaigns against western Native Americans, resulting in more than a thousand engagements.

A. Federal Military Campaigns Against Western Indians

In 1871, the federal government stopped seeking treaties with various Native Americans groups as part of a more aggressive effort to subdue the natives. In the Southwest, clashes continued after the Civil War. In 1875, Apache leader Geronimo was tracked down and momentarily surrendered. The 1867 treaty with an alliance of Plains Indians did not last long because of railroad expansion. In 1868, General Custer butchered a Cheyenne settlement led by Black Kettle.

Indians attacked surveyors, supply caravans, and military escorts that preceded railroad work crews. In 1874, General Custer went into the Black Hills of the Dakotas in unceded Indian land. Although supposedly off-limits to whites, Custer announced that Indian lands were filled with gold. By 1876, 15,000 miners had flooded into Indian lands. Finally on June 25, 1876, Custer and 264 soldiers attacked 2,500 Sioux and Cheyenne at the Little Big Horn River in Montana. Foolishly attacking without backup, Custer and his men were destroyed.

The western Indians struggled to preserve and adapt their lifestyles. Despite brutal repression, Native American culture survived and sometimes flourished.

B. Postwar Western Labor Problems

The Central Pacific Railroad expanded eastward from California in 1865. Although subsidized by the government, the railroad had trouble keeping workers, so in 1866 the Central Pacific imported thousands of Chinese men. These Chinese workers amazed whites with their hard work and skill while working for only $1 a day. When a strike by 5,000 Chinese workers broke out in 1867, it was broken when the railroad cut off food supplies. By 1870, 40,000 Chinese lived in California, representing 25 percent of all wage earners.

Landless California Indians were deprived of hunting/gathering lands and wracked by disease and starvation. By 1870, California Indians had decreased from 100,000 to only 30,000 in a twenty-year period.

C. Land Use in an Expanding Nation

The Civil War had caused new conflicts over land use while making old disputes worse. White Southerners easily kept their land, but Hispanic land titles were at risk of being ignored by Euro-American settlers. In the 1870s, over 80 percent of original Spanish land grants in New Mexico were wrested from their original Hispanic landowners.

The growing railroads made it possible to mine minerals profitably and also spurred the growth of cattle ranching. Railroad connections between the Midwest and East made it profitable for Texas cattlemen to drive herds to railheads in order to ship cattle to stockyards in Chicago or St. Louis. Between 1865 and 1890, as many as 10 million heads of cattle were herded north from Texas. The cowboys who drove them were not all white, as a quarter of them were African American and 15 percent were Hispanic.

Federal land policies were vital to pulling together regional economies. Land use laws had a mixed legacy. For example, the Apex Mining Act of 1872 legalized traditional mining practices in the West and contributed to wholesale destruction of certain areas. Naturalist John Muir fought for the federal government to regulate land use and create a national park system. In the late 1860s, the Pullman sleeping car helped encourage tourism, which pitted tourist interests against those companies that profited from destroying the wilderness.

D. Buying Territory for the Union

U.S. Secretary of State William Seward bought Alaska from Russia in 1867. For about two cents an acre, the U.S.A. gained 591,004 square miles of land that would provide fish, timber, minerals, and waterpower. In 1870, some Republicans joined Democrats to call for the annexation of the Dominican Republic. Charles Sumner blocked this effort while arguing that it was immoral not to consider the wishes of the Dominican people.

III. The Republican Vision and its Limits

The Republican vision of a government-business partnership faced two problems: persons agitating for civil rights and people attempting to reap personal gain from political activities.

A. Postbellum Origins of the Woman Suffrage Movement

After the end of the Civil War, the middle class continued to grow. Many of these middle-class Americans, particularly Protestants, felt a deep cultural tie to England. One belief of America's "Victorians" was the ideal of domesticity—a happy family living in a comfortable home and guided by a pious mother and paid for by a successful businessman father.

Still, the Civil War only made some women more anxious to participate in politics. Many thought they deserved the vote. In 1866, Elizabeth Cady Stanton, Susan B. Anthony, and Lucy Stone founded the Equal Rights Association to fight for the rights of women and African Americans.

Frederick Douglass devoted himself to black male suffrage and left women out of his call for equal rights. African American activist Sojourner Truth warned white women not to claim to speak for all women at the same time as she told black men not to fight only for themselves.

The National Woman Suffrage Association was formed in 1869 to fight for married women's property rights, liberalized divorce laws, and admission of females to colleges and trade schools. Victoria Woodhull was expelled from the organization because she pushed for more radical causes such as free love, legalized prostitution, and labor rights. In 1872, Woodhull formed the Equal Rights Party and ran for President. Susan B. Anthony tried to vote in this election to test the law but was arrested.

B. Workers Organizations

Growing wealth did not necessarily help workers in either agriculture or industry. In fact, many working people fell ever more deeply in debt. In 1867, Oliver H. Kelly formed the Grange, which promoted farm cooperatives and fought unfair railroad rates that favored big business.

Founded in 1866, the National Labor Union (NLU) formed a collection of craft unions and had as many as 600,000 members by the early 1870s. The NLU promoted reforms like the eight-hour day. Although the organization favored "consolidation" of black and white workers, they defended excluding blacks from leadership both in the union and on the job.

In 1873, a nationwide depression destroyed the NLU. Another organization emerged to fight for labor: the Knights of Labor. They aimed to unite workers in industry and agriculture, self-employed and wage workers, blacks and whites, men and women.

Depression led to the rise of the Greenback Labor Party in 1878 that fought against the withdrawal of paper money from the economy, since this made debts harder to repay. Although they had many reasons to unite, workers faced difficulties in building coalitions. A major problem was how employers divided the laboring classes by ethnicity, religion, and race.

C. Political Corruption and the Demise of Republican Idealism

The new government-business partnership led to an extensive system of bribes and kickbacks. Boss Tweed's Tammany Hall political machine in New York City used bribery and extortion to fix elections and steal millions of dollars until a *New York Times* exposé led to Tweed being arrested and convicted. Another example of corruption was Credit Mobilier, which gave Congressmen stock to gain influence.

The federal government seemed ready to withdraw from the South and hand freedpeople over to unrepentant rebels. The presidential election of 1876 saw Republican Hayes out-polled by Democrat Tilden in the popular vote, only to have Hayes become president after he promised an end to Reconstruction in the South.

During the dozen years after the end of the Civil War, the northern Republicans remained in control of national economic policy while white Southern Democrats re-established their control over local and state governments.

Identification

Explain the significance of each of the following:

1.   Freedmen's Bureau:

2.   National Labor Union (1866):

3.   Wade-Davis Bill:

4.   Vigilantes:

5. Black Codes:

6. Thirteenth Amendment:

7. Civil Rights Bill (1866):

8. "Scalawags":

9. Ku Klux Klan:

10. "Forty acres and a mule":

11. Knights of the White Camelia:

12. Charles Sumner:

13. Tenure of Office Act:

14. Command of the Army Act:

15. William Tecumseh Sherman:

16. Union Leagues:

17. Geronimo:

18. Lieutenant-Colonel George Custer:

19. Central Pacific Railroad:

20. Timber Culture Act (1873):

21. Apex Mining Act (1872):

22. Pullman sleeping car:

23. John Muir:

24. William Seward

25. Elizabeth Cady Stanton:

26. Equal Rights Association:

27. Sojourner Truth:

28. National Woman Suffrage Association:

29. Knights of Labor:

30. Tammany Hall:

Multiple Choice Questions:

1. Which of the following was NOT welcomed by Sea Island blacks in 1862?
    A. Teachers
    B. Missionaries
    C. Boston investors who wanted to re-establish cotton production
    D. None of the above.
    E. All of the above.
    Page Reference: 460

2. The Wade-Davis Bill would have required
    A. the North to allow the southern states to leave the Union.
    B. African Americans to take a loyalty oath before voting.
    C. a majority of southern voters to take a loyalty oath.
    D. African Americans to emigrate to Africa.
    E. None of the above.
Page Reference: 460

3. During Reconstruction, President Andrew Johnson
    A. believed that blacks should continue to toil as agricultural laborers.
    B. thought that no pardons should be given to former Confederate soldiers.
    C. never vetoed legislation passed by Congress.
    D. agreed to take on the debt of the former Confederate States of America.
    E. resigned to avoid impeachment.
Page Reference: 461

4. Former Confederate leaders moved swiftly to reassert their authority and passed laws that
    A. reduced the number of men becoming ordained ministers.
    B. instituted a system of near slavery for African Americans.
    C. prevented former slaves from working for white employers.
    D. attempted to send former slaves back to Africa.
    E. All of the above.
Page Reference: 462

5. Soon after the Civil War ended, southern white terrorist groups launched a campaign
    A. that lacked enough money to fulfill its mandate.
    B. that quickly died out from lack of support.
    C. and had to face determined resistance from white plantation owners.
    D. that was not supported by very many southern whites.
    E. of violence against freedpeople who resisted the demands of white planters.
Page Reference: 463

6. The sharecropping system that developed in the South after the Civil War
    A. allowed landlords to exploit poor farmers.
    B. was applied exclusively to African Americans.
    C. established a particularly favorable situation for single women.
    D. was fair to both laborer and landowner.
    E. was applied exclusively to poor whites.
Page Reference: 464–465

7. Which of the following is NOT true about the Freedman's Bureau?
    A. The Bureau compiled a mixed record.
    B. They set up elementary schools and distributed food.
    C. The agency never had the staff to do all the things it wanted to do.
    D. It lasted for decades and was always very well funded by Washington.
    E. The biggest challenge was to try and set up a new economic order.
    Page Reference: 466

8. In response to growing white violence, Congress passed the Reconstruction Act (1867)
    A. to end the military occupation of the southern states.
    B. in hopes of preventing blacks from voting in federal elections.
    C. to purge the South of disloyalty once and for all.
    D. urged on by the most conservative (States' Rights) wing of the Republican Party.
    E. to preserve the "supremacy of the white race in this Republic."
    Page Reference: 469

9. Reconstruction-era southern state governments were
    A. almost all made up of African Americans.
    B. no more corrupt or incompetent than those in the North.
    C. for white men only.
    D. opposed to public school systems.
    E. targets of northern resentment against big business.
    Page Reference: 471

10. In 1871, the U.S. government policy towards Indians was
    A. to grant control to Native Americans of the Great Plains region.
    B. more aggressive with the practice of seeking treaties renounced.
    C. so mild that the Army was unable to launch attacks against the Plains Indians.
    D. to respect the Native American religious belief system.
    E. to basically ignore them completely.
    Page Reference: 474

11. By 1870, 40,000 Chinese lived in California and
    A. they had equal rights with whites with those rights guaranteed by the Burlingame Treaty.
    B. they formed a social and political alliance with African Americans.
    C. they were divided about equally male and female.
    D. found work in a great variety of industries from shoe making to gold mining.
    E. Chinese were never discriminated against by employers.
    Page Reference: 477

12. Hispanic workers
    A. were paid more than native white workers.
    B. became upset in 1867, asking that Irish workers be dismissed.
    C. mainly had worked on railroad construction out east.
    D. were excluded from the U.S. by the Alien Control Act of 1868.
    E. were the primary unskilled labor force in Los Angeles.
    Page Reference: 477

13. Political corruption
    A. existed only among the Irish Democrats.
    B. was mainly limited to the black-controlled state governments in the South.
    C. was engaged in by greedy politicians of both parties.
    D. was almost unknown within the Republican party.
    E. was a result of rejecting a new partnership between politics and business.
    Page Reference: 486

14. Which of the following was NOT welcome in the Knights of Labor?
    A. Lawyers
    B. Black workers
    C. The self-employed
    D. Shoe makers
    E. Railroad workers
    Page Reference: 485

15. The presidential election of 1876 saw
    A. Democrat Tilden receiving the majority of votes from citizens.
    B. Republican Hayes becoming president.
    C. the "Compromise of 1877," which ended Reconstruction.
    D. All of the above.
    E. None of the above.
    Page Reference: 488

MAP QUESTION:

After looking at Map 15.3, discuss what the presidential election of 1876 reveals about regional voting patterns. What accounts for the disputed areas in the South? Compare and contrast with more recent presidential elections.

ENVISIONING HISTORY

Explain how and why different artists depict the Battle of Little Big Horn so differently. What does this say about how different people have interpretations of the same facts?

THE WIDER WORLD

After studying the chronology of when women got the right to vote in various nations, discuss the significance the different dates have for showing the nature of the different societies.

INTERPRETING HISTORY

Explain how the southern labor contract preserved the power of the landowner. How would YOU have felt if you had been presented with a contract like this and told to sign?

CONNECTING HISTORY

Evaluate the key differences between the impeachments of Andrew Johnson and Bill Clinton.

Answers to Multiple Choice Questions

1.	C
2.	C
3.	A
4.	B
5.	E
6.	A
7.	D
8.	C
9.	B
10.	B
11.	D
12.	E
13.	C
14.	A
15.	D